*I want to thank my husband. Roger, this book would not be possibl[...]
loving me with the best love ever. My heart belongs to you[...]*

*Christian, I love you son. And, I love the life and ministry that Go[...]
started at KU. This book is for you, and for all my grandchildren t[...]
prophecy over your life come to pass daily that your identity was assured long ago. Thank you [...]
me to always return to my rock and to remember who I am in Christ. You are my reason and my anchor
and you are powerful beyond measure. Remember, son, your voice is chosen for this generation. Use it
boldly, wisely, and with love. Being your mom is still the best thing to ever happen to my life. Thank you
champ. And, thank you for all the brothers and sons you've given me!*

*Mario, I love you and I love being your mom. Thank you for choosing me and for allowing us to be your
parents. Your smile had me at hello and every time I see it I'm happy. You will have all that you dream and
influence others to reach higher.*
*Amir, I love you and am so blessed by your love in return. I never get enough of you son. After daddy I am
your biggest fan. Thank you for calling me mommy. It makes my heart soar.*
*Jordan, you were an answer to a prayer that has only gotten better and grown fuller. I love watching you
become a young man of God. Thank you for letting us be your spiritual parents.*
*Lubbock, you're an awesome warrior for Christ. Keep being the leader you are son. I love you and Yana to
pieces!*
*Tarik, thank you for letting me be mama and now G2. From our very first conversation you were welcome
inside my heart...and home.*
Maurice, I love being part of your growth in Him, son. Thanks for always laughing at my silliness.
Eric, never forget that God is real and He really loves you! So do I. Just trust Him!
Ryan, you have always been Pastor Ryan. Any mom would be proud! You're amazing!
*Deandre, you were the first and you're forever! Our home is always your home and my heart is always
your heart. You think we can watch the Kardashians together in Heaven? First, let me get the girls saved
and living for Jesus, son. LOL*

*To all my other Kansas, KU Basketball sons, especially Thomas (T-Rob), Perry, Jamari, Landon, Brannen,
Kelly O, Andrew Wiggs, Andrew White, Jeff Withey, Tyshawn, Travis, Elijah, Merve (Swerve), Justin Wesley,
Naadir, and to all the many wonderful, young men of God, who have shared our home, our hearts, our
faith, and our prayers. You are are all warriors for the King! May you walk daily in your identity as you rest
daily in my heart.*

The only thing as sweet as you boys are all my GIRLS!

*Sarah Buschini-Jueneman you pushed me into my destiny in ministry simply because you cared for the state
of affairs of your sisters in Christ. Isn't that how it should be?! May the fruit of our labor bless your home,
and mine, forever!*

*To all my DAUGHTERS. Diana, Bianca, Kiera, Mykala, Sarah Boltz & Mikaela, Sheronda, Kristy, Jade,
Lindsay, Brogan & Caroline...And to all the rest of the furry woodland creatures from KU that made our
home more beautiful! You know who you are! This is for YOU! I love you!*

*Lenny, THANKYOU isn't a big enough word. You have always let me walk in my identity by daring me to be
even more. As we continue to journey together I am so blessed to call you my brother. You mean more to
me than is possible to express here. The beautiful thing is that I know you already know!*

*Finally, last but not least, mom I love you so much! This book is mostly for you. You've challenged me my
entire life to walk in my identity as a winner! Because of you, no matter how bright or how dim the future
may ever look, I know that I truly am a DAUGHTER who is loved.*

COPYRIGHT PAGE

Published in the United States by *SpiritualChick Publishing*

Jenni

No more fears!

Cynthia

CONTENTS

PRODIGAL DAUGHTER

So she got up and went to her father.

"But while she was still a long way off, her father saw her and was filled with compassion for her; he ran to his daughter, threw his arms around her and kissed her.

"The daughter said to him, 'Father, I have sinned against heaven and against you. I am no longer worthy to be called your daughter.'

"But the father said to his servants, 'Quick! Bring the best robe and put it on her. Put a ring on her finger and sandals on her feet. Bring the fattened calf and kill it. Let's have a feast and celebrate. For this daughter of mine was dead and is alive again; she was lost and is found.' So they began to celebrate.
Luke 15:20-24

1

WHO ARE YOU REALLY?!

"We will not hide these truths from our children;
we will tell the next generation
about the glorious deeds of the LORD,
about his power and his mighty wonders"
Psalm 78:4 (NLT)

Our true Identity as sons and daughters of the most high God has been completely lost in the world today. It's been robbed, stolen, and hidden in a myriad of ways. Over time its been replaced by lies. Lies told to us by television, movies, magazines and media. Lies told to us by governments and institutions. Lies told to us by other people. Sometimes, lies even told to us by our parents, friends, and loved ones, who themselves, sadly, believe the worlds lies.

I must state as my dear brother in Christ, Chad Norris, stated, "social media has ushered in a celebrity spirit to the church in the West." This spirit is causing us to root our identities in the wrong things. By its very nature, the number of likes and thumbs up a person receives on a photo, a sermon, or a thought they express drags them into a place of 'self' that is really dangerous. Affirmation of this fact seems to lie in the new trend of many young pastors saying they are called to 'Hollywood.' This calling seems to involve the pursuit of fame, stardom, and worldly validation, as the definition of a successful identity. Worse, its becoming the definition of a successful ministry.

I have worked for many years in Hollywood in the entertainment industry. I was blessed to enjoy the trappings of worldly success. In the end, I realized there was a shallow, hollow, void that existed inside all the money, fame, glamour, wealth, and privilege and I opted, no begged, for God to let me use my talents in the Kingdom.

At a certain point, I screamed out to Him for my real purpose and my true identity to be revealed. I knew it had something to do with my faith. Although, I really had no idea what it meant to be part of the Body of Christ or to live for Jesus. I just wanted to make the world a better place and raise the bar on Christian entertainment because in my thinking it didn't have to be so…well…cheesy.

So, I eventually ran from Hollywood for a season in hot pursuit of Jesus and didn't care if I had a career to go back to. I wanted out of the shallow and into the 'deep.' Deep for me looked like the Kingdom of God and I jumped all in. Leaving my Hollywood state of mind meant something really simple, yet very profound, in my identity discovery. I didn't need the validation, or the affirmation, of the likes and the thumbs up anymore. This was a glorious moment of freedom to be sure! When your identity is so clear to you that you don't need fame, stardom, or even success, to know you're awesome you will step into a realm of freedom, peace, and joy experienced by far to few people in the western world today.

Yet now that I am quote unquote here in the Kingdom I am amazed by how much traffic is going the wrong way on the freeway. There's a mass exodus of people in the Kingdom, some born and raised in it, all with Kingdom knowledge, Kingdom parents, Kingdom calling, Kingdom position, and Kingdom education and family, trying to get into… Hollywood. All, while still keeping one foot in the Kingdom, of course. They then imagine that this is success! Now, in possession of the Promised Land, they desire position in Egypt. Remember, this didn't work so well for the Israelites. They got wiped out with each alliance they made with the land of their former slavery.

Everyone, it seems, wants to be in entertainment. As if Christian entertainment doesn't need you, and the gifts God gave you. Love is needed, and love expressed creatively, through your gifts, would feed the entire planet. They're not gifts that were created by you, and they certainly aren't gifts that belong to you. They're His. As a believer, I gotta say in all honesty, Hollywood doesn't need you as an equal. You don't have enough life experience with sin, and many times not even enough experience with Jesus, to even begin to speak to Hollywood. So what's the deal? Why the pretense that Jesus is calling you to Hollywood? You don't need a like, a thumbs up, or a famous person that you've discipled, to sing your praises. Or do you?

For from the least of them even unto the greatest of them every one is given to covetousness; and from the prophet even unto the priest every one dealeth falsely
Jeremiah 6:13 (KJ)

Honestly, I smell identity struggles even in the body of Christ. And, when the struggle exists the door is open for what my friend, Robby Dawkins, calls the 'identity thief' to come in and make you over into what *he* can use, while causing your true identity to be hidden, even from yourself.

Our Father is wealthy beyond measure, more powerful than any force we will ever experience, and kinder and more loving than we could ever imagine in our wildest dreams. We have inheritances and promises that are waiting for us to claim. A virtual treasure chest of riches is within our grasp and He guarantees us a life lived without limitations or barriers to stop us. This is the good news that Hollywood desperately needs to hear and see *us* walking in. This is the good news that will never be duplicated, replicated, or subjugated, by Hollywood, by Christians, or by any other thing known to mankind. This is the good news that the majority of people today, including Christians, who look to social media, fame, and living in a Hollywood state of mind as the example for *us* to follow, need to wake up to realize once again.

When I look around the world today I see brokenness, lack, and fear driving the lives of millions and millions of people daily; Christians and non-Christians alike. I too have been driven by my own brokenness versus my God-given identity. My fears compelled me to do things I never thought I would do. My focus on my own perceived lack, robbed me of everything I ever gained, or hoped to gain, until I came face to face with my own death and rebirth into the power and success that are my birthright. I too have been lost to who I am and looked to Hollywood; to money, career, sex, and fame to provide my identity.

Until I met my Father, and realized He had amazing plans for my life, I self-sabotaged, chose wrongly, and ended up with nothing time after time after time. All I ever needed to do was get to know Him, which in turn helped me to know myself. By letting Him truly be the good Father that He is I've grown more and more powerful, achieved more and more success, and become happier and happier day by day; even in the midst of challenges and problems and life's daily battles. We live in the world and as Jesus said; in this world you will have tribulation! However, as is written in Philippians, we are more than conquerors through Christ who loves us. And, Christ loved us enough to have died for us in order to overcome the world.

So why the lack, fear, confusion, and brokenness? Why the utter demonic destruction in the lives of hundreds of millions of Christians worldwide today? Don't we know better?

Why the chaos and struggle that seems to rule over you?

Why the unhappy endings and the broken fairy tales and the financial debt that passes from one generation to the next?

The answer is as simple as it is complex. Broken Identity. We've lost our identities, if we ever understood them in the first place.

We don't know who we are!

We have no idea what it means to be a chosen generation.

We don't know how to be in the world but not of the world.

We don't understand the power of being a 'peculiar' people, rather than one of the bunch. Instead we value being like everyone else, and chasing the same things everyone else is chasing, because walking our own individual paths, as Christians, seems so unpalatable, unhip, and uncool!

For the non-believer all of this is understandable. But for us believers, it's as if we've been given the keys to an amazing Kingdom that we want to hide our membership in. Understandably worse, our brothers and sisters who have revealed themselves as Christians, have done such a poor job of representation that many of us would rather cringe and hide from any exposure as related to them, than say out loud in a room full of people, 'Hey guys I'm a servant of Christ and He loves you.'

But I am! And you are! And He does!!!

It's time to look at your life and grow into your future embracing your identity as the son and daughter that you actually are!

2

A CHILD OF THE TUBE THAT'S ME

But I am afraid that as the serpent deceived Eve by his cunning, your thoughts will be led astray from a sincere and pure devotion to Christ.
2 Corinthians 11:3 (ESV)

Losing my identity started with the world's favorite pastime; television.

Like many Americans, I grew up a child of the tube. It's no doubt I would go on to work the many years I have in TV, because my love affair with the tube began at a very early age when appointment viewing was everything. It meant a great, fun, night of family shows like The Brady Bunch and The Partridge Family in my home. Television was not really harmful back then. We all need only watch some of Nick at Nite to realize that we've fallen very far, very fast, in terms of what we have access to in the media.

By the time I was in my early 30's I was a full-fledged member of the church of Sex And The City. I believed in the casual affairs of the heart, mind, and body that it flaunted. I lusted after Carrie's Manolo Blahniks, her career success, a man as powerful as Mr. Big, and a larger apartment on the Upper East Side, with the right friends who also lived at the right addresses. This was, after all, real life, in the real world, as created on TV, and endorsed in magazines. So, I thought. So, I believed. So, I lived.

My media brainwashing started off on a pretty good diet of family fun, which allowed me to escape the dark secret occurring in my home; my childhood sexual abuse at the hands of a relative who lived with us.

TV was innocuous. It was fairly harmless, as was most of what was available to us in terms of media back then. At the risk of sounding old it's actually shocking that I never saw nudity or inappropriateness anywhere near prime time. Eventually, TV provided me the power I needed to escape the abuse that came against me, once again, as a teenager that I silently endured.

Over time television actually provided a training manual for the many different characters and behaviors I could try on, and hide the brokenness of my abuse, behind. I learned about sex, and marriage, and passion, and men, all from TV, movies, and magazines. I grew into becoming a young woman, and while I was a Christian, my faith was really only a part of me. I was not really a part of it.

Like many, I had no real grounding in truth. So I gave myself to various forms of media to teach me about life. TV, while at first a savior for an innocent little girl, whose innocence was being silently stolen, became a training manual for Satan to groom me into the confused, rebellious, woman I would become. The many 'How To' articles I read in Cosmopolitan Magazine served as my 'How To' guide to life. How to be a better sex partner, How to please your man, How to dress for success, How to do your hair, your makeup, and your faith, were the many lessons communicated to me as the Word for my life. I went to school devouring the world's truth, at an alarming rate, as nearly every young girl I know, and knew, did.

Robbed of any answer to the questions, 'who am I' and 'why is this horrible sexual abuse that no-one knows about happening to me,' I would look for many, many, years to magazines, books, TV, and movies to tell myself, and therefore others, who I was, and why I felt what I felt. And, who I was could change as often as the television channel. *I held the remote control and when I pushed the button I could switch the channel instantly to a new identity.* Simply put, while it served to protect me, and help me cope, it was exhausting.

Much like in the film, The Matrix, we are plugged into a system of lies. It's not until you break free from that system that you realize that *everyone* is plugged into the lies and only after you've unplugged are you walking in the truth. By unplugging from The Matrix you can see it for what it is; a necessary system of control when you don't want people waking up to the truth. Especially, if that truth frees you to understand that your real identity is rooted in God's power, love, beauty, and freedom.

We have been completely deceived, just as Eve was deceived in the garden, into thinking that if she did something that was *less* than what she already was, she would be *more* than what she already was. God made man and walked with man in the garden. He was there to answer every question His Son and Daughter had; yet they chose to turn to devices to get the answers without Him. Eve ate the apple to possess all knowledge of herself, and the world around her, when all she had to do was ask her Father. So it is today. We look to books, movies, magazines, people, and social media, to provide the answers when all we have to do *still*...is ask our Father.

Satan's game has never changed. He hasn't had too. We keep falling for the same old tricks. Usually those tricks come wrapped in the form of something exceptionally beautiful and pleasing to the eyes or tasty to the flesh. Your enemy, Satan, never comes as ugly as he is with the game he's playing obviously displayed. I dare say we might figure it out and walk away if that was the case.

No, your enemy will always come as an angel of light; good looking, cool, and sexy. He will come in the form of your favorite TV show and the really sexy new movie that is rated R but should be rated X. He will validate you with the constant barrage of photos that tell you, that guys need to see your butt and breasts to actually engage with you. The images will be glamorous and beautiful; but your demise is certain.

Those images may be moving and sometimes even spiritual; but if you don't have a relationship with Jesus you'll be left powerless. Then, once you are hooked, which takes about 15 seconds, Satan can get you to do, or sell, nearly anything; your soul, your position, and ultimately your real identity, for more of what he offers. Whatever we think will work to fill the void and eliminate the lack we will barter away if we don't know who we really are.

3

MEN, MEN, & MORE MEN

They are the kind who worm their way into homes and gain control over gullible women, who are loaded down with sins and are swayed by all kinds of evil desires
2 Timothy 3:6 (NIV)

For me, the greatest area of identity confusion came in the form of men.

I was so scarred by my secret abuse that I entered my twenties really unsure of what it meant to be loved or desired in any real, or healthy, way. I built substantial walls and reclaimed my power by forming an ability to hurt before I got hurt. The media diet I ate fed me the power to own my body, by using it just as men had used it. However, the perception of power lay with me because I was the one doing the using and not them. Was I happy deep down inside? At times I could convince myself I was. But I wasn't really. I intuitively knew that I wasn't made to be casual about sex and that I wanted more; although I didn't think I deserved more. Sadly, the constant double mindedness we experience in our brokenness, especially as women, works to keep us in a state of confusion that blinds us to the truth of what God intends for us in men.

The Word tells us our enemy is the ultimate deceiver of the brethren. Well, let me tell you, he is definitely the ultimate deceiver of the sisterhood. We girls can be sooo...easy!

We open the doors to our hearts, our souls, our minds, and our callings, time, after time, after time. Only to get knocked out by pursuing the wrong thing to fill the identity void yet again; guys, money, sex, fame, clothes, status, youth, bigger breasts, lips, butts. All of it is designed to gain attention and be valued; mostly by men! We consume makeup like water, hair extensions like crack, and whatever else we can consume to make us become the identity that we see projected at us from a hundred different directions.

Instead of looking inside for our *true* identity, especially when the Holy Spirit lives in us, we look outside at books, magazines, and TV shows to teach us what to do, how to act, and what to wear to snag a man. We try and become a smiling portrait of someone who must be happy and successful because she's famous, has a child in her arms, and is on the cover of a magazine. Our identity doesn't require much searching to find, because if we just read the right materials and dress the part appropriately, or inappropriately, as is the standard today, then we can win, win, win.

Why look inside when it's so easy to find identity outside?

The truth is, we know what's inside, and it's often ugly and painful and we don't wanna go there. Inside is Pandora's box and opening it may unleash a world of problems, issues, and brokenness, thereby projecting the honest truth about what our real identity is, instead of the false identity we wanna project.

Since most times, before knowing our Heavenly Father, the image projected inside our box is not pretty, nor does it paint a picture of the happy, desirable, successful girl we want the world to see, we just avoid the box and therefore we avoid letting God heal everything that exists inside it. We remain hidden inside, trying yet another makeup trick, fashion device, or guy choice, that will project the image of the identity we are crafting for ourselves.

I have nothing against hair extensions and makeup but I also enjoy when I take the hair extensions out and wash the makeup off and still feel awesome about...ME!

The problem with keeping the lid on Pandora's box is that it's basically the same as choosing to remain plugged in to The Matrix. Choosing to remain blind doesn't eliminate the reality that there is much to see if you open your eyes. And, while the view may be ugly and painful initially, if you let God inside your cluttered box, He will show you great things that will heal your pain and transform you into the uber daughter or son you were born to be. He will make good on His promise to give you beauty for ashes.

In Eve's deception, she was doing more than innocently trying to fill a need or a void, with the wrong thing. She was hoping to become equal with God. To have His knowledge. In some sense she wanted to control Adam by using her power and influence over him in all the wrong ways. It actually cost her the comfort she was seeking. How many times do we see this same pattern today?

How many times do you stop and really look and realize that we haven't stopped being deceived by Satan one little bit? We surely haven't stopped deceiving each other at all. And, the power of this game is destroying the very lives we seek to live today. There is only so long you can fake everything about yourself. Even if you don't know you're faking, and even if others don't know you're faking, it's easy to be so lost that you're walking in deception daily and living a life that you've constructed of hair, makeup, clothing, and guys to define you.

I know because I did it. I know because one day I woke up in a nightmare of lost identity, confused identity, broken identity, stolen identity, and didn't know who I really was at all. I was so many different women. There were even songs to back up my broken, fractured, identity as glamorous, so I figured, what the heck. I'm every woman. If you can't beat 'em. Join 'em. So I did. I joined them until there was nothing left of my identity at all. The less I understood about my identity the more I looked to the world to provide one. When I finally realized it couldn't, or worse, would provide me with one that was completely inconsistent with my beliefs and with what I KNEW was right in terms of God, it was time to walk away.

4

RICH DAD POOR DAD

For our earthly fathers disciplined us for a few years, doing the best they knew how. But God's discipline is always good for us, so that we might share in his holiness
Hebrews 12:10 (NLT)

My dad's name was Bernard Garrett, Sr. My moms name is Linda Guillemette Garrett. They met in a bank where my mom worked when she was 18. She thought he was the most handsome man ever. He was tall and dressed better than most men in his custom made silk suits and alligator shoes. She also thought he was the most intriguing man ever judging by the swagger he walked with, the amount of money in his bank accounts, and the total confidence he possessed. All of which served to deny his humble Marlon Texas, uneducated, background.

In spite of very little formal education, and certainly no legacy of contacts to help him, my father became the first African American man in our country to ever own banks. He owned seven white banks and savings and loans scattered throughout the, at that time, very racist state of Texas. This was quite an accomplishment for a high school dropout, and black man in Texas in the sixties, when coloreds couldn't even ride at the front of the bus or drink from the same water fountains. My dad and his business partner, Joseph B. Morris, used to disguise themselves as a chauffeur and a janitor to obtain entry into their own board meetings.

My dad's partner, whom I called 'Uncle Joe,' was an educated black graduate of UCLA. Their story is documented in part by famous celebrity attorney, Melvin Belli, in his book My Life On Trial. Mr. Belli eventually defended them against the federal government in a case that changed banking laws in our country forever.

Theirs was a case that likely would have never happened if Joe hadn't loved the spotlight so much. He reveled in their success, and loved appearing on talk shows, rather than just enjoy the life of privilege they were living right under the noses of a very racist country at a very turbulent time in our history.

My father preferred to fly under the radar never allowing others to know who he knew, where he lived, or what he had. A lesson I still walk in today.
"Baby girl, let people be stupid enough to underestimate you. Never have so much pride that you can't silently allow their small minded ways of thinking bring them down while your knowledge of yourself brings you up." Incredible advice from a man with little formal education.

I remember wondering, as a small girl, why when he would go to work collecting rents, or meeting workers, at his various properties, he would wear the overalls he wore and drive a beat up old car or van, when he normally wore custom made beautiful suits, expensive shoes, and drove a brand new Cadillac with a car phone in it. It was all about not drawing attention to the fact that he was living as Blacks weren't supposed to live, according to white men, in his mind. His small town roots in Texas had taught him that this type of display of wealth fostered envy and racism, which only drew trouble. He preferred to avoid trouble and live the way he wanted.

He was surrounded by privilege in his life by the late 60's and early 70's. His circle of friends included Sidney Poitier, Muhammad Ali then known as Cassius Clay, Harry Belafonte and others. He had many white, Jewish, and Italian friends, never really caring about color, even though it had often been used against him.   He was often ringside in Las Vegas at Ali fights in a fur coat and hat like all the wealthy black men in his day.

My dad was a strong, silent, visionary. He never once in his life touched drugs, did not get drunk, and quit smoking cigarettes in his thirties by placing a pack in his suit pocket for a year. He never once lit one up. He said after a year he knew that he had mastered what tried to master him and he tossed the pack away and never looked back.

My dad raised us with the belief that, while he came from nothing, had little formal education, and was discriminated against in the worst ways for his skin color, you could do anything if you worked hard enough and didn't give up. He used to say to me, "Slim, you're a victim for the first twenty minutes someone does you wrong. After that, you're a d*mn fool! You gotta take the hand that life gives you and play it! Play it well."

This lesson would carry me through the worst victimizations of my life.

Eventually, because Uncle Joe went on a talk show and talked about the millions they had, and the banks they owned, he and my father were indicted on trumped up bank fraud charges. In spite of then President Lyndon B Johnson's attempts to help bail them and their banks out, they sat in a high level security prison called Terminal Island for a year while Melvin Belli was given all my dad's real estate holdings, assets, and money, to get him off the charges. My father walked, the laws changed, and Belli owned everything my father had worked so hard to acquire. Part of those holdings included a good chunk of what is now downtown Los Angeles.

Many years later, I was given a letter of guaranteed employment with the lofty Belli Law Firm in San Francisco upon graduation day from law school. This guaranteed employment helped walk me right in to the law schools of my choice.

My dad would stand again, and he would even rise, only to be clobbered by the Bahamian government after, then Prime Minister, Pinland, invited foreign investors into the newly liberated country of The Bahamas. Working with all black men seemed so appealing to my father after years of racist battles in America. Sadly, once he turned an ailing business into a thriving resort, and boating marina, on the island of Freeport, Pinland nationalized his businesses. That basically means he took all his money and his business holdings and invited him out of the country without recourse.

My mom was told she could stay. Since my father wasn't Exxon or Mobil Oil the U.S. government wouldn't intervene and that was that. My father's work was dashed again.

I was to young to understand what was going on, but I do remember that this experience was the nail in the coffin on years of stress and tension in my parent's marriage. The night my father left the island my mom sat in bed with all six of us small children and cried. I had never seen her cry, which worried me very much. I sensed great trouble and turmoil as my father, who was devastated, left. Broken once again by things I didn't even understand or comprehend as a small girl.
My mom simply said, "I'm sorry but I don't love your father anymore. It's not that I don't love him. I just don't care, and that's worse." We left the island days later and their marriage was over.

Because of my dad, and his words, I never chose to be a victim. This quality has served me and saved me many times in my life. It's fundamental to faith actually. There are no victims in Christ. There are only overcomer's. He was certainly one. Knocked down by adversity many, many, times he always got back up and he died trying to stand.

My mother, never a victim herself, has been no stranger to adversity either. In almost an instant my brothers and sisters and I were off of the island and living in a small desert town called Barstow, California with my grandparents. My mom took a job in Los Angeles saying she had to get on her feet and build a life for us and then we would move in with her full time. With that we were left waiting for weekend visits, which sometimes didn't come, once my young mother found a boyfriend and a life as a single working woman. Making the drive in traffic to Barstow was often prohibitive of my young mother coming home on weekends. Those weekends were always the hardest of my life. I've never asked my sister and brothers what they thought because I've always assumed much of their dysfunction today stems from these difficult years. They were so young. To be stripped of both parents was horrible for me; I can only imagine what it did to them.

5

MOTHERHOOD

My son, keep your father's command and do not forsake your mother's teaching. Bind them always on your heart; fasten them around your neck. When you walk, they will guide you; when you sleep, they will watch over you; when you awake, they will speak to you.
Proverbs 6:20-22 (NIV)

Everything I learned about motherhood I learned from my mom.

Linda Marie Guillemette, married very young. She was strikingly beautiful and still is. She gave birth to me when she was only nineteen. I learned in my thirties that I was actually the glue that kept my parents together in the middle of a divorce after only one year of marriage.

My parents first year was turbulent. She was young and beautiful. He was old fashioned, handsome, rich, and possessive. He also had another woman with whom he was involved when my parents initially met. Hers was a name I heard again through the years as I got older and overheard my parents fighting.

They eventually decided to amicably divorce and go their separate ways. In the court room, documents ready to be signed, the divorce terms already negotiated and agreed to, my mom picked up her pen, and in nothing short of Oscar worthy drama, pretended to read the documents one last time before signing. She looked up, puzzled, and innocently said, "Oh no! I can't sign these!"

My dad erupted. Both parties legal counsel sighed. The judge was frustrated when he asked, "WHY?"

My mom, all of nineteen years old and stunningly beautiful took the entire court proceeding by surprise when she flatly replied, "Because there is no provision for my unborn child!"

The attorneys spun in a circle facing her, while my father sat down with his mouth wide open. That child was me.

They reconciled and stayed together seventeen more years and five more children. Their bond of love, friendship, and admiration, never really died. My dad took it to the grave as will she, I am certain.

The fate of their rocky beginnings ended in a fairly easy divorce decision, made on that warm Bahamian night, seventeen years later, however. My mother never sued my dad or took him to court. She told him plainly, "Bernard, You gave me six kids that I wanted. If you want to help take care of them that's great. You're their father and I trust you will do what you can when you can. If not, their mine and I will."

With that, my mother never said a bad word about, or against, our dad. She always understood when he didn't have enough to help because yet another visionary business failed and she always understood that he would do what he could when another visionary business was having some success. She loved him till the day he died, as he loved her with even his final breath. They remained friends and respected each other always.

I am still moved by her display of grace and dignity as a mother. After raising my own child, I am even more aware of her love for us in not bad-mouthing our dad. Sadly, every other woman seems to paint her ex-husband into a monster, in a play to make the kids hate them, as much as they do. Even if the woman's goal isn't to make the child hate his/her father, the simple bad-mouthing causes all kinds of mental issues and challenges for a child to overcome. Love wouldn't do this. I am, so grateful she cared enough to let me have my own relationship with my father. I am so grateful I was left to make my own decisions and formulate my own opinions about him, independent of hers.

My mom was big enough and wise enough to realize that kids needed to think the best of their parents for their own development to be less fettered by issues. Even if it's all a fantasy in the mind of a young girl, that her dad is Prince Charming, I cannot understand why any woman, if coming from a place of love, would steal that fantasy from the heart and mind of her own child. Knowing that dad loves you, and that he is a good guy, is foundational to how young girls, and boys, develop. How do parents not see that teaching kids to forgive and to see the best in the other parent is often the only way they can mature enough to actually deal with the eventual revelation of parental imperfection?

I am saddened by the experiences I've seen, even personally, where women have used kids as pawns to trap guys into relationships they may or may not want, and guys recklessly make babies, with various women, as badges of honor for living thoughtlessly and carelessly. There is often so little knowledge today, and even fewer financial resources, to understand how to raise children or how to support them. An absence of God as Lord of our lives has caused much devastation to God's intentions for family today.

It's pretty clear to me that our families have been destroyed because we have taken God out of His place as head of the family. We serve ourselves and our selfishness instead of God. The irony is that He actually serves us, and blesses us, if we serve Him.

I have no doubt in my mind that children, no matter the circumstances that bring them here, are blessings from God. We are to steward them wisely or we will answer harshly one day for our poor shepherding of their lives. They are to be wanted, loved, and supported at the sacrifice of self. I have moved many times, worked many times, and passed on adventures many times, because of my son. Not once did I feel a sacrifice was made that deprived me of something I wanted more. Nothing compares to him.

No child asks to come here. And, it is my firm belief, that parents OWE them a chance at life. Period. I have very hardcore conservative and honest views about parenting because I have lived to see the good, the bad, and the ugly, from parenting when it's great and parenting when it's not so great. The kids pay the price for poor parenting and ultimately society pays the price.

We have to raise our kids as believers and provide the knowledge they need to not perish in a world of confusion and hopelessness. I see, today, entire generations that have searched out answers, in drugs, alcohol, and sex, that are so easily found in the Word of God.

This is not my parenting book so I won't elaborate here on the things that I have learned parenting my son who turned out miraculously well, once I surrendered my entire life to The Lord. I will say this, however, my mother taught me to always be a mother and not seek to be a friend. I learned from her that if I did my job well, friendship would follow. The place I learned to do my 'job' as mother well was in the Bible. It contains wisdom needed to navigate the honesty with ones self, and the instruction and discipline needed to navigate raising children today, yesterday, and forever. Generation after generation, as we get further away from embracing our Judeo-Christian values and leaning on God to guide us as people, knowledge and wisdom is disappearing from our country and from our world. The Bible teaches us a solemnly simple lesson:

"My people are destroyed for lack of knowledge"
Hosea 4:6 (KJV)

Suffice it to say, that when I became pregnant with my son years later, the role model I had already had of 'mothering' was good enough for me to decide that at any cost this child would know God's love and support, and feel loved and supported by me, all the days of his life. This commitment has been aided, supported, and divinely navigated by a total surrender to Jesus Christ as true Lord of my life. Yes I made and make mistakes. Plenty of them. I just make them with a desire to serve God and please Him always in view. This brings me to the place I can say to my son, 'I am sorry' or 'I was wrong,' when need be. I try not to wear masks and to be as transparent as possible with my son in parenting him. After all, kids know and intuitively understand most things. You cannot fool them. They see you and they see your inconsistencies when you're living in them. Being honest with them about your strengths, weaknesses, successes, and most importantly, your failures, serves to destroy the works of the enemy that creep in when compromise, inconsistency, and mistakes go left un-confronted and un-apologized for. Most times young people just want you to be 'real.' There is such freedom in your honesty as a parent for you and for your child. I have seen the living victory of the Word that says

"Then you will know the truth and the truth will set you free"
John 8:32 (NIV)

Being truthful also means recognizing the individuality of your child. It is absurd to hide from the fact that as a parent you have to deal differently with each child you have. Kids are not all the same, just as people are not the same. We can come from the same household and have wildly different viewpoints, needs, and personalities, because God makes us wildly different and because kids process their environments and the things that happen to them in those environments differently. I was raised in a home where my siblings experience of a particular relative was extremely different than mine, because I was sexually abused by him, as was my sister. This colored my emergence from our same home in many different ways with many different consequences. I was different based on the environment I was experiencing.

My mom, while far from perfect, did an amazing job of supporting us as the individuals we were. I always felt that someone had my back and I still do. This gave me the confidence to try anything I dreamed of trying throughout my entire life. Oddly, I inherited fearlessness from my parents that, when coupled with my mothers support and encouragement, helped me to live the life I wanted on my own terms. What she didn't have was adequate knowledge to know how and why I needed God to save me, to teach me, and to instruct me. Things I had yet to discover about God, whom I always believed existed would be like water in a dry, dry, land when I finally stepped out of ignorance and victimization into knowledge and wisdom.

My parents gave everything they could to nurture my identity with all the tools, and knowledge, they had. What they didn't provide was an understanding of my identity as determined by my Creator. So, my curiosity and my search, as with many, drove me forward. The need to know who I am, and why I am, propelled me up many mountains, into many valleys, and into various forms of hell, yet to be revealed.

6

BARBARA WALTERS REALLY?!

But now, O Lord, you are our Father; we are the clay, and you are our potter; we are all the work of your hand.
Isaiah 64:8 (ESV)

As I've mentioned, I was hugely drawn to Hollywood and the pursuit of fame, stardom, and worldly success to be specific. However, I lacked understanding of identity as I now see identity today so I assumed that if I could have all of what I thought would make me important and desirable then I would be just that; important and desirable. I remember seeing The Shawshank Redemption as a young person and sitting in the movie theatre as tears rolled down my cheeks praying, "Please God, let me be a part of this world of making films. Let me create beautiful forms of media to express the human spirit." I wanted in. I wanted to express my real feelings.

As a child, I often pretended to be Barbara Walters. I was exiting a private plane and rushing to interview some foreign dignitary or movie star. My red carpet dreams weren't just dreams to me. They were the source of my inner focus, and my determination, in ways I now see few people ever experience. I felt that I knew what I was born to do and I had a clarity about it that often surprises even me.

As a young child, I stayed awake at night sneaking to turn the lights on and read books all night long. I would get lost in my imagination and sometimes not come out for days at a time. Movies and TV shows had the same effect through the years, but not back then. As a young girl, it was books that I got lost in. I loved to imitate characters and try on personalities. I was completely immersed in fantasy and loved the escapism of it all. My mom would often have to come in my room and make me put whatever book I was reading away and go to sleep because I had school in the morning. I would literally hide under the covers with my dad's flashlight and continue reading when she left the room. I didn't care that I would be exhausted the next morning. If I were lost in a good book, and a world I wanted to live in inside it, I would pay the price to extend my fantasy for as long as possible. Sadly, I was using make believe to escape the reality of my life and the fact that I was being sexually abused by an older relative. Barbra Walters was an *ideal* I created to escape an ugly *reality*. Inside my mind I found characters I could lose myself in and hide in. I didn't like to come out. When I came out of my fantasy world I didn't understand why what was being done to me was being done. It was confusing and scary. I knew what was happening was wrong yet I didn't understand what I was supposed to do. So, I did nothing, for fear of *what* I didn't know.

This single event would color the rest of my life. This is where my heart broke, before our home broke, along with my parent's marriage. This is where my soul literally split and I learned in a very deep way that life was a battle spiritually and a literal warfare against our spirits exists. I was nine years old and I was broken.

Prior to nine years of age, I don't really remember my childhood. I have a couple vivid memories of events that hurt me, or marked me, like threatening to run away one night at about six years old, or the little girl who lived near us saying she could fly as she stood on the balcony of a third floor building that we lived in at the time. I don't remember if she jumped or not. My mom told me that she did.

Besides these pre-abuse memories, however, I have no real memory of my family being a family and having fun. Oddly, my memories all begin around the time of my sexual abuse; the good ones and the bad ones.

Life began with a real awareness and preparation of what I understand now, better than many, because it's been an important area of spiritual study for me. Understanding what felt like a very personal war against my spirit from the time I was a small girl has been the greatest discovery of my spiritual life. The only thing greater, truly greater, infinitely greater, has been the understanding that God loves...ME!

7

SPIRITUAL WARFARE

"Finally, my brethren, be strong in the Lord and in the power of His might. Put on the whole armor of God, that you may be able to stand against the wiles of the devil. For we do not wrestle against flesh and blood, but against principalities, against powers, against the rulers of the darkness of this age, against spiritual hosts of wickedness in the heavenly places. Therefore take up the whole armor of God, that you may be able to withstand in the evil day, and having done all, to stand. Stand therefore, having girded your waist with truth, having put on the breastplate of righteousness, and having shod your feet with the preparation of the gospel of peace; above all, taking the shield of faith with which you will be able to quench all the fiery darts of the wicked one. And take the helmet of salvation, and the sword of the Spirit, which is the word of God; praying always with all prayer and supplication in the Spirit, being watchful to this end with all perseverance and supplication for all the saints."
Ephesians 6:10-18 (KJV)

When I read this scripture for the first time, with real understanding, nearly 20 years later, I was overwhelmed with a depth of clarity and purpose that resonated to my very core.

All of a sudden, the knowingness of God settled upon me. Some call this a revelation, an epiphany, a knowing that you've found truth on a level that is beyond human words. It doesn't matter what you call it, or how you call it, this passage above explained my whole life. I finally found the explanation of what I knew in my spirit from the time I was a child. The state of mankind's actual existence here on earth is that we live in a state of spiritual warfare.

We are all God's kids, called by God to serve Him. Yet, sometimes, Gods kids get used by the enemy, even unwittingly, in the war that is waged here against us.

God's enemy hates God and all that is Godly; including His children. He wages war against our very lives to stop us from ever walking in the power of why God wants us to know Him, and to live for Him. God's word is truly a lamp unto our feet and as we follow it we go from victory to victory in Spirit and in truth. This terrifies the enemy of our very souls. It terrifies him as much as the day he, Lucifer, realized Jesus Christ had taken the keys to death and opened a door forever out of his trap.

My war was not against humans. It wasn't against my relative who sexually abused me. It wasn't against the two young men who raped me at 15. It wasn't against even those who in my mind lied to me, abandoned me, abused me, or used me. My war, all along, had been against the enemy I felt in my spirit when sometimes someone entered a room and I instinctively knew they were bad. You know the feeling you get when you can tell someone dislikes you for no reason or is threatened by you without any apparent cause?! I knew that real enemy.   That spirit of evil, jealousy, strife, or confusion that I often felt on people or in situations or events was real; as real as God is real I know Satan is real. He uses our weaknesses and fears against us and against others and only through standing in faith, with the knowledge of how to put him in his place, do we prevail.

In my experience, even we Christians don't like to discuss Satan and spiritual warfare. It's scary to some, and uncomfortable to others, to acknowledge the existence of a deity that is pure evil who holds court in this world wanting to destroy us constantly. He is the opposite of our Father. Yet, his existence was very real for me.

After the truth of Ephesians the single greatest books I ever read, were The Screwtape Letters by CS Lewis, and This Present Darkness by Frank Peretti. The fact that others understood the realities God showed me as a child, even before I knew scripture, has been incredibly validating and useful. When you've walked for many years with a truth, and an understanding of things, that you didn't know anyone else thought about or knew about, and those things are then explained and validated by others, it is profoundly liberating and powerful. Liberating, because it's a huge relief to know you're not crazy but in fact, simply, the only one in your immediate world who has been given an important revelation in response to your questions and confusion. Powerful, because you now know the depth of the truth God has revealed to you, which validates not you, but Him, and opens the door to a huge question. Why did you show me this truth God?

My entire life bears witness to why I was given this truth so early on. He allowed me to understand Him and spiritual warfare so deeply because I am used constantly to help others identify it in their own lives. The teaching He does through me is equipped with an anointing of purpose and revelation that far out-measures my intellect. Only God's supernatural ability can make complete sense, of utter nonsense and chaos, to a child. Only God can sustain that child well into adulthood until he or she can understand that it was the supernatural ability of God all along providing for him or her. Only God has the mercy, love, and patience to wait for that child's inner revelations to catch up to adult understandings, in spite of the confused acting out that the child indulges in trying to explain their confusion to himself or herself. Only God. Why?

Because He had a plan. Because He has a plan.

We win, always, if we walk in the Spirit with the armor described in Ephesians above. We have a very clear and simple set of instructions for victory so that the same lies and deceit our enemy has used since the beginning of time will not triumph over us.

We wrestle and war with demonic attacks of all sorts, using people all around us, even our loved ones. We are taught in the Bible, in more ways than solely in this passage in Ephesians, that our fight is not against these people. It is against evil spirits and a hierarchy of ranking bad dudes. But we win by putting on our armor daily. As a Roman soldier prepares for war, Paul explains the dressing of our spirit, body, and mind in the armor of God that defeats our enemy at every turn and in every battle.

...Therefore take up the whole armor of God, that you may be able to withstand in the evil day...

We are not told to put on one piece of armor. We are told to put on the full armor. A soldier wearing only ankle shields will likely get pierced through his chest when the attack begins. His enemy knows where the weak uncovered places are. Your openings are visible to your enemy when you are at war. He knows how to win. You better know how also. Or you'll lose. Then you become the cliché that blames God for your lack of being armed properly, even after you've been given a clear set of instructions.

...and having done all, to stand. Stand therefore, having girded your waist with truth...

After you've done everything to arm yourself with truth, i.e. the knowledge and wisdom He provides in His Word, stand and wait in faith that your God did not give you incorrect or bad instructions. As any soldier does, you put on your armor, take the field of battle, and wait for your enemy, knowing you're fully equipped to win.

...having put on the breastplate of righteousness...

Your righteousness is in Christ Jesus. It's why we all need a Savior. Prior to Jesus none were righteous and without Him none are righteous. He died for us to be seen as righteous before God. This acceptance of Him covers your heart. It heals your heart. It protects your heart. The first thing broken in an attack is our heart. The breastplate covers a soldier from being pierced in the most vulnerable place on his or her body when at war. An arrow through the heart kills. This piece of armor is essential.

...and having shod your feet with the preparation of the gospel of peace...

Having you yourself repented, you are then prepared everywhere you go to share the gospel of peace. You will rid the environment of much warfare by bringing God into every room you enter. People have many replies to many things that make sense. I rarely see anyone have a reply to the truth of God when delivered by a soldier who really knows and understands who God truly is and what His word truly says. This is why the lack of knowledge of the Word that runs rampant in the church today sickens my stomach. We are at war and have zero depth of understanding for how to fight it. Instead we focus outwardly fighting people. We sound like immature, ill equipped, representatives of a weak and powerlessly confused God, rather than carriers of an uncompromised truth and undefeatable warriors of an almighty General. I look around me at young women today and I am amazed at how unattractive their lack of knowledge really is. I am deeply saddened by the simple truth that they themselves are clueless as to the fact that they choose moment by moment to venture in uncovered by God, clothed in shame, and prime for slaughter by the enemies many disguised motives and clever deceptions.

...above all, taking the shield of faith with which you will be able to quench all the fiery darts of the wicked one...

Every soldier uses his shield to deflect arrows from striking him. Our faith is our shield. Faith displayed in action against the enemy's attacks is faith that eventually wins the war. Our faith may weaken in a battle, or even be non-existent in one battle versus the next, but our faith will eventually reveal, even to us, our victory. The wicked one, your enemy, will attack you. God isn't hiding the ball. Life isn't a rose garden. It has thorns and worms in it. But even a rose was given thorns to protect itself, just as we have been given armor, if we choose to wear it, to protect ourselves

...And take the helmet of salvation...

The helmet covers your head. Your mind is where all wars take place. I remember the revelation in my spirit when I first heard Joyce Meyer say, the battlefield is the mind. I've come to understand this fragile yet fertile place where thoughts and ideas, good and bad, can take root and grow into all kinds of things great and small. Diseases or cures, blessings or curses, all take root in the mind. Your salvation is your faith and acceptance that Jesus Christ died for your sins. This has saved you. Your salvation is your helmet. It protects your mind. Know whose you are, and what you believe, and your mind will be protected time after time by the amazing grace of your salvation, which has been assured by Jesus.

...And the sword of the Spirit, which is the word of God...

The sword is what you pierce your enemy with. The sword delivers the mortal blow to an enemy's heart. The sword is the soldier's weapon. In one hand he uses his shield but then in the other hand he wields his sword to strike and kill his enemy. The sword of our spirit is given to us directly by God and the more we know of it the more we can use it effectively to destroy the attacks and works of our enemy against us. The Word of God Himself is our sword. It's not just His Word it's His Rhema word. That means his word spoken out loud. There was a time I used to walk through my home saying scripture out loud until an attack on my spirit, which was waging itself inside my mind, ceased to be effective. I didn't even realize then that I was engaging a piece of my armor. I was using His Rhema word to fight. It worked every single time. It works every single time. The choice is yours, however, as to whether you will stand in faith and pick up your sword and fight, or retreat into a world of defeat, chaos, confusion, and unquestioned unbelief. I see many people choose the latter daily.

...praying always with all prayer and supplication in the Spirit, being watchful to this end with all perseverance and supplication for all the saints...

So much can be said for this simple command. Praying always. For all the saints. One is actually challenged by this scripture, in my humble opinion, to ask themselves the question; do I even care enough to pray always for anything or anyone besides my own laundry list concerning myself?

In our selfish, entitled, millennial age, I dare say that the levels of self-focus, vanity, and pure selfishness that my generation ushered in is now on steroids. People can't even see how vain and self possessed they are. I see a generation of 20-somethings actually self absorbed enough to think they're the only ones asking the questions they're asking, making the mistakes they're making, and experiencing the messes they're experiencing. Even, the age-old journey, of questioning God's existence seems to be something many feel is exclusive to them and their heightened intellectual existence. It would be hilarious if it weren't so tragic.

To think yourself the first ever to question God makes me laugh to my very core. When we become so vain that we don't realize that we are simply the same cliché that happens over and over again, generation after generation, decade after decade, then total self-absorption and pride is running rampant.

What has been will be again, what has been done will be done again; there is nothing new under the sun.
Ecclesiastes 1:9 (NIV)

God has survived our questions, and questioning, since the beginning of man on earth. He is still the biggest conversation and debate in the world and, suffice it to say, that long after we are all gone He will still be the One being talked about.

The enemy is winning on many levels, however, because of the sheer vanity present in the world today. We feed young people today, making the same mistakes I made, a diet of milk and sugar wanting God to be easy and palatable and never wanting them to feel threatened or challenged or uncomfortable because, after all, that's no fun. At times, I want to vomit. Since when did we lose sight of the fact that everything about being spiritually mature, and ultimately successful in any battle, is about feeling uncomfortable and challenged? When did any Roman soldier ever feel comfortable and un-challenged on the field of battle? War is about death people. The sooner you wake up and realize that your very life, your kid's lives, and your families lives are at stake, the sooner you can get to the business of obtaining the truth that saves, sets free, and arms you correctly to win the daily battles that equal victory in the war against your lives.

Prayer, or your lack of prayer, is a revelation of how selfish and entitled you really are or aren't. I challenge you right now. Do you care enough to pray always not just for yourself, but also for others? Do you care enough to pray in a way that engages God with your heart open to what He tells you is right and wrong, and then to follow and act on what you're told? Do you care enough to know that this life is not about you?

Well, whether you care or not, let me tell you quite clearly and without regard to your feelings; it's not about YOU. Life is not about YOU!

I often tell the story of reading Rick Warren's book 'Purpose Driven Life' for the first time. The book sat on my end table for about three years before I opened it. It looked good there. I wanted to be someone who read it. I just never found time. I was to busy with, well, me! Then one day, almost as if a sense of urgency gripped me, I knew I was supposed to get away, alone, and read the book.

The first sentence on the first page of the book destroyed me. I think I experienced a total and complete mental breakdown all in one moment. The sentence read: It's not about you!

WHAAAAT?! OMG!!!!!

Then what on earth was it about I thought in a panic?!

I was raised to set goals and achieve and it was most certainly all about...me and my efforts! Now, I was being told it wasn't about me at all. I had spent my entire young adult life spending time alone, even taking silent retreats, to nurture my spiritual life by myself. This was to strengthen my faith and confidence in...me. I needed to have faith in me because I thought that me was all there was to be concerned with. Now I was being told that it wasn't about me, or anything I thought, or did? I was being told that were created as part of a body and each part of that body needs to function in concert with the other parts in order for the body to have success.

Well, one of the main functions we have in serving each other and functioning at our highest, and most effective, is in prayer for each other. I spent five years of my life as an 'intercessor.' I prayed daily, for hours a day, not just for my son, but also for every child on his basketball team at the University of Kansas where he played. I prayed for his coaches, whom I sometimes hated, because many of their coaching tactics went against every single thing I know to be true about love and mentorship; not to mention good parenting. I prayed for the other parents; the ones I loved and the ones I found impossible to even like. I prayed for the university, the town, and the entire state. I sat for hours a day and prayed. In that state of having my heart submitted to loving and seeing them all as God did, He poured much revelation and understanding into me. He gave me the ability to love them and value them as He does and to forgive them and pray for their growth and spiritual maturity. He taught me to care enough to pray for all the saints. Even for all the saints who often resemble sinners more than saints. The things that were rooted out of my heart in this season of constant prayer opened my eyes to the shocking reality of my own need for constant prayer and forgiveness. There is nothing more powerful to triumph over the enemy than prayer; especially prayers over people you know might lie to your face, talk about you behind your back, hurt your child, and never waste a moment of prayer on you in return.

Our victory, plain and simple, in the spiritual warfare we live in here on earth is found in prayer. We must pray for each other. We must pray for protection and covering from the various forms of spiritual warfare and attacks we all endure around the world daily. Our highest power, as the body of Christ, in my humble opinion, is not about any single one person but about every single person standing in prayer for the next.

In the warfare I experienced in my young life, I always knew that I would win. I always knew God was real. I felt Him and I felt His presence with me as a child. He was good. Before I knew why and how He was good, I knew He was good. I always knew God would look after me, but discovering the fact that there was something contrary to God working against me, helped me to know that I was not alone or crazy.

I, in no way, as warned by theologian and scholar RT Kendall, am making Satan and his warfare bigger or as relevant as the war Jesus wages over us to protect us, guide us, and escort us into eternity. But, how else does a child who knows she is having her spirit repeatedly attacked and assaulted by people, feelings, and things both seen and unseen, understand that God has a tremendous plan for her and that her very existence creates fear and hatred in the heart of Satan? So much so that he will dispatch a team of demonic activity at her to stop her and to thwart Gods plans for her like nothing her worst human enemy could ever achieve on their own!

One must recognize spiritual warfare to understand that they are not unloved by God, but feared by the enemies of God. Just as Satan feared Jesus, we as God's children are hated, feared, and targeted. We must acknowledge that we are at war, in order to fight back, just as much as we need to acknowledge that we are at war in order to know that we are loved and protected in ways to incredible to comprehend.

We wrestle not against flesh and blood, but against powers and principalities that use humans unwittingly, even those who love you, to poke into your deepest wounds and fears and cause you to stop, give up, leave God, and go any direction but the one He has created you, prepared you, and equipped you to go! God is NOT to blame for your pain and your doubt and your confusion. He is not telling you that you're worthless and that you're efforts are stupid and that you should abandon your hopes and dreams. Satan is. Satan uses his warfare, waged in actions, events, and words, through others, to accomplish his goal of stealing your calling, stealing your hope, stealing your joy, and ideally stealing your life and your identity. You have a very real enemy of your soul and only he is to blame for the illnesses of the world and the deception, hurt, and destruction of mankind. Only he is to be blamed for trying to destroy...you.

In beginning God created. In beginning Satan tore down and deceived. In the end, God gave His only begotten son so that whosoever believes in Him would not die but have eternal life, continually being built up and fortified to walk in abundance and victory. We win the war on the spirit if we arm ourselves in the way we are told. There is no fear in perfect love. Perfect love has cast out fear. Jesus is that perfect love and with Him we cannot lose.

Yet, somewhere, after dark memories of dark rooms where things were done to me that I knew were wrong, and after my parents divorced and the stability of my childhood was shattered, I was often left unattended by my mom who had to work to support my five siblings and I, so being raped as a teenager under her very nose was yet another simple attack for the enemy to pull off.

At about 16, Feeling abandoned, completely misunderstood, exhausted, and far to knowledgeable about the weakness and ugliness of men, I was filled with a rebellious fight to make it and prove to the world, and mostly myself, that I was worth something! This desire consumed me and drove me until I found my life and my worth hidden in my real identity as determined by Jesus Christ many years later.

Sadly, however, the war against our value is likely the greatest and most effective warfare the enemy uses. When you feel as if you're worth nothing there isn't much you won't do or engage in.

My sexual abuse, and eventually my being raped, as a teenager were part of the demonic war waged against me to get me to quit on life and people, to leave God and my faith, to go my own way in rebellion, and to get me to take my own life; because after all it wasn't worth much anyway.

For a time, Satan's lies can actually work when you don't know how to war against them.

8

BEVERLY HILLS 90210

Do not be afraid; you will not be put to shame. Do not fear disgrace; you will not be humiliated. You will forget the shame of your youth and remember no more the reproach of your widowhood.
Isaiah 54:4 9 (NIV)

I attended Beverly Hills High School. It's everything you might imagine. Wealth. Excess. Beauty. VIP Parties. We had access to anything we wanted including everything we shouldn't have had access to.

I was in the 'in crowd' and as a cheerleader we lead the pack. By junior year my strength and my ambition was formidable. I had survived my turbulent childhood and become a fighter of epic proportions. Already forged in the fire, my spirit was literally unbreakable. I set my focus on achieving fame, wealth, and status. This was the world I wanted to live in because I thought it would certainly make me valuable. I was desperately seeking value from a world that had actually devalued me in many ways. This is how Satan works; he makes you chase him for what you can never have; value from a world that doesn't value a child of God at all.

I chose to go to law school, but my sights were on becoming a star in television, film, and entertainment. I was super smart in certain ways, always ahead of my time creatively, and possessing a vision of what was 'in' and what was 'cool' that was truly supernatural. I have been told in recent years that my gift of seeing creative trends in TV, movies, fashion, and society was most likely a strong part of a very prophetic gift that I have and now understand.

I have never believed in false modesty because I don't think it's true humility, so I became very confident in myself and my strengths, while comfortably acknowledging my weaknesses. I didn't really need any cheerleaders or fans. I never felt I really had any anyway so I didn't put my faith in people. I put it in God and myself. It's odd, but even amidst this youthful confusion, I still managed to salvage shreds of hope that my identity was special and that God had something to do with wanting me to win because He had carried me through so much evil as a young girl. I didn't really know how or what the significance of my being constantly delivered was, or meant, I just knew He had my back. That gave me the hope, the faith, and the fight to continue pushing toward validation for my significance.

By college, my looks began to blossom along with my confidence and inner determination. I took it for granted that I would be successful and live a certain life. I never doubted that I was born for more than the abuse I had received.

When I look back I realize I ran over a lot of people in my brokenness and my need to protect myself and prove my worth. I was so determined not to let anyone ever hurt me again that I actually hurt others. My relationships were quite disposable in a way. I could leave anyone and move on with little connection to feelings, theirs or mine. I was deeply broken in this way yet the ability to protect and guard my heart was also a God given blessing, and a tool. It is an ability many people, who've been deeply hurt, are given from a very young age. It enables you to proceed forward until a time of understanding and healing can actually be had. Like a soldier whose leg gets shot off on a battlefield, shock takes over, and the soldier doesn't actually feel pain immediately. The pain will come; but not right away.

I always had the best looking boyfriends. They were the ones that everyone wanted and no other girl could tie down. I had a pride in this fact, which was also about me proving my worth and showing everyone what my 'identity' was. I never really settled down with any one guy. I just paused for a time, in a moment, or a season if things were more serious, before moving on to the next chapter. My heart was in a box. I would love only me. And God. Although, God was still just a distant friend, whom I took with me everywhere, instead of the other way around.

As much as I walled myself off from men hurting me, girls presented a different discomfort for me. I experienced my first forms of female betrayal in high school. The couple girlfriends that hurt me, hurt me deeply, so I shut most of them out quickly. Girls were dangerous to me, because I didn't expect women to hurt other women. When I discovered they actually did, it broke the code in my mind. So I recoiled really fast and really hard from close bonds with women. It would be years before I could venture confidently again into relationships, especially sisterhood, with women.

The worst forms of betrayal from women, oddly, came because of men. I found out the hard way that women could be cunning and manipulative because most of them were searching solely for identity in a man. They weren't necessarily dreaming of careers, as I was. They were dreaming of weddings. I didn't have wedding dreams and fantasies. Significance and value, I believed, were ultimately found in career, money, and power, so men were just window dressing to that in my early experiences.

I had long moved on to using men simply for my pleasure while I created the identity I wanted in my career. I remember, years after high school, hearing the audible voice of God tell me that I had a Jezebel spirit on me. It had been there since high school. I didn't know what that meant then but I knew it wasn't good.

Back then anyway, I learned a lot from men about competition and achievement. I learned the dialogue, and the strut, of what it means to confidently pursue your end goal. Not surprisingly, I gravitated to athletes from as early as my high school years. The sheer, raw, arrogant, confidence they employed to win was super attractive to me. I had no time for the limited game I felt that women played. To me, men were simply far more interesting to navigate. They were driven by success, and materialistic achievement, and every now and then they needed sex without complications and that made perfect sense to my broken self. Sadly, once you added up the variety of ways in which the enemy had used guys to break my heart, summing up their identity in such a shallow way became as simple as that. I understood this, and therefore them, and I liked that they were easy for me to fathom.

Or so I thought. Until law school. And River.

9

RIVER

Then you will be handed over to be persecuted and put to death, and you will be hated by all nations because of me. At that time many will turn away from the faith and will betray and hate each other, and many false prophets will appear and deceive many people. Because of the increase of wickedness, the love of most will grow cold, but the one who stands firm to the end will be saved. And this gospel of the kingdom will be preached in the whole world as a testimony to all nations, and then the end will come.
Matthew 24:9-14 (NIV)

Suffice it to say, I had lots of guy friends. I was one of the guys, and while every bit comfortable in my skin as a girl by my college years, I was always more comfortable with the guys. An odd reality given my background and lack of real trust in men. I shut down the part of me that a man could really hurt early on, and the ambitious, no time for mental games, part of me was all guy. I was competitive, brash, and uber confident, as were only one or two of my girlfriends, so I embraced being a guy's girl. I also loved being able to control guys when I knew they wanted me. In my experiences, guys took what they wanted when they wanted it. So I did too. I was uncontrollable, so in my experience men desired me. A desire rooted in their innate need to conquer, I imagined.

But then along came John, aka River. For better and worse he was my male equal. We met in college while I was dating my high school boyfriend. He and River attended Stanford University. Riv was brilliant, popular, handsome, and athletic and we were fast friends.

There is always one for whom all the walls drop. River was that one. We were alike in so many ways, good and bad. He was as elusive as air yet as present as skin when we were together. There was something magic and charming about him. He had a strength that reminded me of my own. He had a charisma that was so electric, ambition that was so unbridled, and a love of excess that was so decadent, that we eventually consumed each other. It was almost as if we both knew we had met our match in each other. The word soul mate seemed to describe what was otherwise inexplicable about our connection.

When my high school boyfriend and I broke up after college, while I was in my second year of law school at USC, River and I started spending time together daily.

We would just hang out. For the simple pleasure of being together we would take long drives through the canyons and mountains and along the ocean around LA. Of the many conversations we were having, we discussed much about life, and death, and miracles. River was diagnosed with cancer, during this period. Hodgkin's lymphoma to be specific. It was found in a lymph node in his neck while he was in Colorado training with the US Olympic cycling team. Cycling was something he began in his college years to rehab an injury after he couldn't play basketball anymore. I will never forget the day he walked into my apartment in West Hollywood with his head shaved bald and a look of bewildered strength in his huge doe like eyes. He looked at me and smiled, sheepishly insecure as to what I would think about him shaving his hair off because of what the chemo and radiation was doing. I don't think I ever loved him more, or deeper, than in that moment.

It didn't take long for him to confess that he liked me better than our mutual friend, who was also my ex. Sadly, my ex became some of the wreckage caused by his two broken friend's desire for each other, and the lack of boundaries that came with that brokenness. I didn't need any convincing to move forward with Riv because the writing was on the wall in the form of the deep mental connection we shared, the even stronger physical attraction we had, and an intense spiritual awakening that was calling us both. The combination of feelings was so palpable it overcame me in a way I had never experienced before in my life. Amidst our own fleshly desires, interests, and sin that I didn't even realize the enormity of, we were also beginning to seek Jesus together. The mixing of all of this was a recipe for disaster that I didn't comprehend at all back then. This is often something I see when young people fall in love and mix their growing relationship with God as part and parcel of the relationship.

River's parents were amazing Christian people. They had been married for many years, were financially successful in worldly terms, and as spiritually mature, steadfast, believers, they lived their faith in their actions. They helped and loved others. They stood on Gods word for all kinds of breakthrough. And, they always had a Christian channel called TBN on watching some funny and engaging preachers that I began to really like. When I was in their home it represented everything I had never seen in mine and everything I wanted mine to be. I loved being around them and with them. They were like oxygen to me.

The sincere reality of this good-looking, amazing, African-American couple was an inspiration I chased after with my whole heart. I felt God was trying to lead me in a right direction and for the first time in my life I let my guard down and allowed River into my heart. I opened my mind and myself up to him. I allowed myself to see my life with him, and him alone. In my mind, we would be like his parents and that was perfect to me. We were partners in friendship, partners in love, partners seeking more spiritually, and partners sexually. Why wouldn't we be partners in life? I took it for granted that we would, so we naturally began talking about homes and marriage. I accepted a total vulnerability with this guy who could literally complete my sentences and read my thoughts. He knew what every look meant and every move had meaning that only he understood. I gave myself completely to him.

My brother, and best friend, Lenny, once jokingly said the two of us made him sick because, we were so in sync that in a room of two hundred people there was always only he and I. Our eyes were always locked and checking in with each other through a sea of people. I felt that he completed me in the sense that he was truly the beginning of me and the end of me. He was my best friend. I had finally met an equal, mentally, spiritually, and physically. Our ambitions were firing at the same speed and in the same direction; up. We were an explosion of synchronicity. We made perfect sense together. And, I was sure that's how God intended it.

Sadly, we were also both completely broken and in need of inner healing in ways it would take me another twenty years to fully comprehend. Underneath the surface, neither of us was equipped to handle what we were feeling at all. We were, however, sincerely trying.

We had been going to church together, as influenced by his parents, and were dealing with a growing awareness that our relationship was mired in sin. We were having a very complex physical relationship while experimenting with drugs like marijuana and cocaine. Our conversations were turning more and more toward how to stop the spiritual high we *thought* we were on, in order to get on a real one. However, we had little experience, or understanding, of The Lord and His place in our lives, or in our relationship. We just knew we needed to break the mold we were in. But, the more we discussed the need for breaking where we were, the more insecure and fearful of losing what we had we both became. The enemy had us in a complete state of deception and we sensed it. We were opening doors through mixing drugs and sex and didn't have enough spiritual maturity to understand how we were destroying the relationship God had blessed us with.

On top of everything else, as he recovered, and his cancer was cured, he needed to know if the spiritual seeking he had been engaged in with me was really his desire, or his parents and his illness talking.

He also eventually revealed to all of us that he had a young son that he had fathered in college that we never knew about and he needed to move to Northern California to be a father. My life was in LA, however, so his weekend trips became a thing I dreaded, knowing I could never argue that he should stay with me and not go see his child.

When we broke up it was as if someone hit me in the gut with a truck. I was sideswiped, even though I saw it coming. Reduced to calling random numbers that appeared on the bill of my car phone I discovered my worst fear. I found out he was cheating and I was devastated by his betrayal. I had never experienced what I myself had dished out in the past and it hurt like crazy. It hurt so badly and so deeply that in reality, I couldn't breathe for years. At that time, I literally couldn't get out of bed for weeks.

I remember calling, my other brother and close friend, Robbie, daily for what seemed like months crying and crying and crying. Robbie, like Lenny, was a brother and friend who occupied an influential, role in my life. These two friendships, from high school, have lasted till today. Honest and pure, I thank God for the nurturing and love I've received from these two brothers of mine through the years; especially back then when what I experienced with River may have caused me to kill myself. I felt that broken inside. The perceived abandonment, and rejection that I felt, tapped into brokenness that I wouldn't understand

for years to come. I had built walls around emotions that came from my childhood abuse to protect me and create a safe zone for me to live in and my walls had been breached. I was a mess.
I simply didn't see it coming with Riv. I opened myself up and got killed. Nobody knew this better than Robbie. I didn't show anyone my real, honest, devastation over River because I trusted very few people with the truth. I hid it from the world, to ashamed to let anybody know I'd taken down my walls, and gotten knocked out.

To allow River to have the honest part of me, that I was hiding behind a free spirited façade of toughness, only to be betrayed, threw me for a huge spin. Robbie understood that spin and spent weeks consoling me, as I lay in bed unable to move, eat, or function.

10

THE SPIRAL

I have told you all this so that you may have peace in me. Here on earth you will have many trials and sorrows. But take heart, because I have overcome the world
John 16:33 (NLT)

When River left for good, moving back up North, I was already in a virtual spiral. I was one year out of law school, and trying to pursue my dreams of making it in Hollywood as an actress and a talk show host, and I was struggling to get my life started. To make matters worse, my mom wasn't happy at all about my decision to chuck three years at USC law, and a stable career with a Century City firm.

In hindsight, I have always believed that I had the equivalent of a functional nervous breakdown, although I wasn't functioning very well at all. Very quickly, I began using a lot of cocaine to numb the pain. I would chase it with alcohol to bring myself down enough to sleep. I graduated from casual use to medicating myself daily to deal with the pain in my heart, the disappointment and confusion about where God was in all of this, and the voices that were beginning to tell me there was more to what I was going through than just River. He had opened a chasm, but the wounds were already there. It was as if he had jumped inside a pre-existing hole with salt and vinegar to remind me of the intense pain that existed in the hole in the first place.

In church, alone now, I was crying throughout entire services aware that I was really lost and really hurt. I knew that what I was doing was not filling the void or eliminating the deep pain I was in, much of which seemed to connect back to my childhood, but I felt so alone and confused I wanted to die.

I found a way of putting some walls back up by numbing myself with drugs and a new guy, or two, here and there. I rationalized that at least this was helping me to be able to get out of bed and find my desire to run across the finish line of success again. I wanted to smash my desirability in River's face knowing that they all always come back. My anger and hurt became a prideful need for revenge and rebellion against anything inside me that was nice. The walls went back up, fortified in a new way, and I existed in this wounded, fractured, broken, state of mind until Lenny, who was living with me began to get worried.

He looked at me one day and simply said, "Girl, are you OK?" I knew he was referring to this new affair with cocaine.
"I'm fine. It keeps me skinny and in control." He raised his eyebrows unconvinced. He was right to be unconvinced. I wasn't even convinced. I wasn't myself and I certainly wasn't in control. In fact, I've never been more *out* of control.

The things I did to find my confidence again were crazy. In a voracious quest to construct an identity that said, 'I am confident, desirable, and over River, I ran through famous and wealthy guys like toilet paper. The more status they had the better. It was all aimed, of course, at getting a reaction from him, which sometimes worked, and justified the means to my end.

He was now living in San Francisco and whenever he called to check on me, because he really did love me, although I wouldn't see that for years to come, I shut him down and closed him out by going on about whatever singer or actor was in the space he vacated. I felt I had to act cool and over it with him to salvage some dignity, by reconstructing whatever walls had once been there that he had breached. For all my pretense it wasn't working because when we hung up I cried, did a gram of coke, and pushed myself mindlessly through the moment.

I was a wreck, and feigning an independent, it's all good friendship, with him only made it worse. We women always do this. Instead of admitting that the last thing we need, or are able to do, is be in relationship, with a failed relationship, we pretend, suck it up, and fake our way through the agony of defeat and failed expectations. It's as if keeping a toxic relationship in our life is better than not having it at all.

This, of course, set the perfect stage for the man I met who, while being the catalyst by which I was destroyed, would also be the catalyst by which I was saved.

11

AN IDLE MIND

Idle hands are the devil's workshop; idle lips are his mouthpiece.
An evil man sows strife; gossip separates the best of friends.
Wickedness loves company—and leads others into sin
PROVERBS 16:27-29 (TLB)

Bored to tears one night, I went to the grocery store to buy stuff to make pasta for Lenny and I. As I roamed the aisles I noticed two unattractive, unkempt, European guys in soccer gear and sneakers fresh from a workout were following me. Red flags waved inside me. I wasn't impressed or interested so I avoided eye contact and kept moving.

At the check out counter I thought I had escaped them only to turn around and realize they were now in line behind me. The one who had been pressing the hardest reached in my basket and began helping me unload my items. I gave him a hard, cold, stare, which clearly said, I don't want you or your help, so he smiled and backed off.

I paid and went to the black, convertible, BMW, the law firm that recruited me from USC law school had gotten for me. My interest in the car lasted longer than my interest in practicing law so I kept the car, took over the payments, and drove it proudly, while pursuing my childhood dream of being a talk show host. It all looked so together on the outside. On the inside, I was stressed because I couldn't pay my bills, my mom was supporting me, which was a huge struggle for her, and my efforts to make it in Hollywood were not going well at all. My financial instability provided additional fears, doubts, and confusion, on top of everything else that was already rumbling under the facade.

I reached back to retrieve my last bag and as I turned the guy was standing there holding my bag with a big grin on his face. His buddy stood silently behind him.

"I just wanted to know you. In my country we say hello when we want to know someone."

"Well, in my country we don't have to say hello if we don't want to know someone." I was agitated.

"C'mon. My friends and I are meeting in Beverly Hills for a coffee and drinks after dinner. It's a large group. I will write down where we will be and maybe you come meet us."

If I had any hope of leaving the parking lot I figured I better at least take the information that he wrote down on a piece of my paper bag.

12

THE LEADING OF THE HOLY SPIRIT

For all who are led by the Spirit of God are children of God.
Romans 8:14 (NLT)

So, if I were walking in what I know today is the actual leading of the Holy Spirit then every instinct inside me that said "STAY AWAY" would have been heeded as the clear voice of God protecting me.

But, on that night in my mid twenties, I was lost in the great identity crisis of our time; I did not know what it meant to be a child of God, an heir to a throne, a Daughter of a King, a Bride of Christ, worthy of every good thing, and deserving of purity. Absent true identity, after a life being broken by Satan's schemes and plans, it is virtually impossible to have the self-esteem necessary to navigate the world today. But even more, it is virtually impossible to have the full understanding of how to navigate your own issues.

I am amazed at how many people tell me they don't hear God. I didn't think I actually heard from Him either, but I did. I just didn't give Him the place of authority He should have had, because I didn't realize at all that my true identity as His daughter assured that He had been speaking to me my whole life. I thought I could feel Him affirming my decisions at times, possibly through events or circumstances, but I certainly didn't think He was taking time from Heaven to speak to...ME! I didn't really believe I was that...important. And, at the times I did believe I was that important, I didn't have the faith or the understanding to recognize that God was actually speaking to me all the time.

That statement strikes me as tragic because I find it to be true for so many. Whether or not you have children you may understand it better in this way. How important are your kids to you? What would you not do to protect them and guide them and assure they have amazing lives? What would you not do, what mountain would you not move, to communicate with your child whose lost, and lonely, and needing to hear from you desperately?! If you answered, not much, like most people would, then it's an easy stretch to ask yourself; what would God not do for us, His kids?

I believed that it was God who orchestrated many things to protect and guide my life. But, I have to believe, that if I had enough foundation to KNOW that it was God, and enough self love to think I was worthy of His love, I would have listened. I simply had no clue about my identity in Christ, or what that was, much less where to find it. Satan, my enemy, had done a very good job of destroying my self-esteem, stealing my self worth, and causing me enough self doubt to need constant validation from people and things that don't matter at all to my actual identity.

By the point in life, on this particular night in West Hollywood, California, I had been robbed in so many ways, as we all are, of the correct forms of love, validation, and stability that the events that surrounded my youth told me I was as worthless, as the events that surrounded my life told me I was great. This duality sets the stage for why we hear so many competing voices in our minds.

The two platforms screamed opposing views into my life so loudly that when the enemy jumped in through circumstances and events, like sexual abuse, rape, parents leaving me feeling abandoned, fear for my future, sadness, pain and anger etc. the negative voices, sadly, were the ones that dominated. This is how brokenness works together with spiritual warfare.

This is why I try to be gentle with others, as they make mistakes that seem like such obvious mistakes to me, as a more mature believer now. It is virtually impossible to know the depth of someone's brokenness and the reasons that drive the often crazy behaviors and choices they make. This is precisely why so much scripture tells us that God is merciful and kind and slow to anger and rich in love.

The LORD is compassionate and gracious, slow to anger, abounding in love.
Psalm 103:8 (NIV)

He is patient, as any Father is, with a child whose struggling to figure it all out. And, His mercies are truly new every morning. They have to be. If you've raised kids you know that patience, mercy, wisdom and love must rule every moment of parenting, because kids make messes.

In a moment of boredom I was about to make a big one.

It is true that many people just don't listen to even their own instincts, much less to God, if they even suspect He exists and that it's, quite possibly, Him speaking. I cannot imagine God saying go left and I choose right at this point in my life. Going against God's instructions never leads anywhere good. Mistakes are made. Lives are changed. Destiny is delayed if not destroyed. No, today I recognize that God moves and speaks directly to us through circumstances, events, people, and in our own hearts and minds. The Holy Spirit affirms and guides us personally and the more we actually learn to listen and trust Him speaking and ruling our lives the more He will move and reveal Himself as the orchestrator of our amazing journey's.

What happens when we don't listen, whether because of our own will, our own flesh, our own pain and brokenness, our own spiritual immaturity, or even our own rebellion?

Well, I am grateful for God's capacity to relentlessly pursue us even to the depths of hell. He never gives up. He never abandons His own. He never changes. He is the same, yesterday, today, and forever.

And, we know that God causes everything to work together for the good of those who love God and are called according to his purposes **Romans 8:28 (NLT)**

I am quite grateful for the truth stated here in Romans because this promise was about to become the giant hope of my life!

While home cooking pasta for when Lenny came home from the recording studio, he called.
"Hey girl."
"Hey babe."
"I'm gonna work late. Don't wait up."
"Cool." I should've eaten and gone to bed but now I had the night free, nothing to do, and nobody to keep me occupied, so my mind didn't race to thoughts of loneliness, leading back to River, or to my mom who was getting increasingly upset about me not using my law degree and getting a 'real' job. Her words. She was exhausted from my confusion, while at the same time, trying as hard as she could to be supportive of my dreams.

As I lay on my bed, staring at the ceiling, I was drawn to the piece of paper with the information scribbled on it. I picked it up and looked at it for the first time. Miloj, it said. I pulled a white bindle from my drawer. In the silence of my room, I wrestled with my thoughts as the drug took over. It gave me a fake feeling of being powerful and in control. Why not, I thought. I picked up the phone and dialed the number.

I knew the place I was going as I pulled up. A certain type of European frequented it regularly. Euro-trash, we actually called them back then, because there were a lot of unsavory foreigners who hung out in certain Beverly Hills restaurants and bars picking up American girls with money. I figured, in the worst-case scenario, I would not like anyone and leave after a drink, having cured my boredom for the night. In the best-case scenario maybe I would meet some new friends. I loved meeting new ways to distract myself, especially in the form of people. I had so many friends and was generally really social and really liked by people. The noise of people drowned out the voices in my head that were screaming for help and attention. Those voices were telling me that I had problems I needed to confront, that my life was off track, and that I needed a savior.

I had effectively turned the voices off for the night, as I walked toward the bar and saw many people talking and laughing. I didn't see Miloj, which was his name. I stopped and surveyed the scene. As my eyes scanned back to the bar a really well dressed, extremely good looking, guy turned around and our eyes locked. He smiled confidently. It was him. All I could think was; WHAT ON EARTH HAPPENED TO THE GUY FROM THE MARKET!

He looked nothing like the unattractive, unappealing, unkempt guy from the neighborhood market who had trailed me through the grocery store earlier, annoying me to death by his pursuit of me. Now he looked like he stepped off the cover of a magazine. He was drop dead gorgeous! Tall, handsome, sexy. I smiled curiously, while inside I thought to myself, the night just got a lot more interesting.

We took each other in over drinks.

Having never had anything but a worldly relationship to sex, I didn't realize how deeply my abuse, coupled with the absolute lies we are fed in the media and through entertainment, colored my opinions and attitudes about it.

In my efforts to reclaim, and own, my own body and to be the one who said yes to whom I wanted, when I wanted, and not when they wanted, I became very cavalier about sex. I didn't think it had any spiritual implications or effects at all, that were of concern to God, or of consequence to my relationship with Him.

I believed that if I controlled it I was winning over whatever agenda any guy could have over me with it. I was the one with the power if I was able to say yes or no and therefore, I would never be overpowered or controlled by men again. No man would ever rape me or sexually abuse me again if I was the boss. This for me was God. I rationalized that He gave me the power to win, with this thinking, because surely He wanted me to triumph over what was done to me.

This is the line of reasoning sold to us today that I embraced wholeheartedly. My empowered ability to say yes when I wanted, and to pick and choose who and what I wanted, was my idea of spirituality and God blessing me with power.

Yes, I know what some of you may be thinking. Warped? Completely. But, I am not surprised at all to know that this is the dominant way women today justify their sexual behavior; acting out their confusion in what appears to be self empowered, self loving, pleasurable, power over their bodies. The abuse women suffer from birth to their thirties is shockingly veiled and hidden. We are devalued from the day we get here by our current social and spiritual conditions. Our identities are stolen, our ability to even see a man from God's perspective is all but non existent, and we mask deep loneliness and need for partnership behind random moments of false love, fake intimacy, and the pretense of enjoying our sexual freedom.

Armed with the lies that determined my mindsets, deciding as I finished my drink that I would have sex with this man was my decision not his. I vowed after River to never get hurt by love again and I had long since learned that sex was not love. I knew we were attracted. I knew he wanted me. I also knew I wanted him and since I didn't know him, or care about him, he couldn't hurt me in my mind. Simple math, I thought. He couldn't hurt me. Because, I didn't care. End of story.

Problems seemed to occur when you want a story, which, for the first time in my life, I had allowed myself to want with River. I wanted the whole story, the entire fairytale, including God. Wanting the whole story, however, required information that I didn't have, and tools I had yet to acquire.

In reality, the problem is not in wanting the whole fairytale. We should. God wants that for us. The problems occur when you attempt to have the entire fairytale in your own way and not God's. He has a blueprint in the Bible, for right living and for victory, and our issues in the world today are all because we refuse to even try His way, long enough to see that He is right and our way is wrong. Lack of faith, often caused by brokenness, laziness, rebellion, an unclear understanding of identity, and fear of losing the life you think you have or want, all play into why we don't just submit to Gods plans for the earth.

It is clear that since we were created by God to want a 'meaningful, lasting, story' this inherent characteristic about human design will inevitably take over. Only then do the problems with our society, and our warped way of thinking, reveal themselves.

But, on that night, if I could stay rooted in the lie that we could have sex without love, and never be hurt by it again, then I was OK. So I dug down and planted my roots in my perceived freedom to do as I wanted.

13

SEX VERSUS LOVE

It is God's will that you should be sanctified: that you should avoid sexual immorality; that each of you should learn to control your own body in a way that is holy and honorable, not in passionate lust like the pagans, who do not know God; and that in this matter no one should wrong or take advantage of a brother or sister. The Lord will punish all those who commit such sins, as we told you and warned you before. For God did not call us to be impure, but to live a holy life. Therefore, anyone who rejects this instruction does not reject a human being but God, the very God who gives you his Holy Spirit
1 Thessalonians 4:3-8 (NIV)

Because the thinking, that lead me into a number of the wrong open arms, is so prevalent amongst the young women I mentor and counsel in my ministry, I think here is where I will elaborate this point.

Many young girls get so confused in their quest for love by being told repeatedly that sex is not love. Sex is not love. Sex is not love. This is true. The problem is that sex was made for love and women lie to themselves, and to men, when they don't admit that we essentially *use* sex...*for* love. Conversely, men it is said generally use *love* for sex. This fact allows men to tap quite correctly into understanding that it's easier to get the sex they want, if they feign the love we need. And, no matter what girls say love is what they really want!

I believe, that in the twisted and very deceptive sexual lies packaged for us today this is all basically true and representative of the way millions of people now live. So, when a person is deceived, and lying to themselves, believing they don't need love, it makes it easy to fall for the belief that you can use sex *apart* from love.

Satan, the enemy of your life and soul, understands very clearly your need for love. But, his primary objective is to *keep* us thinking that we don't *need* the love that is supposed to go with the sex. If we don't need love, then sex is an easy game of pleasure without any rules. This line of reasoning is ultimately responsible for the destruction of marriage, commitment, family, and anything else associated with God's original design for man and woman.

Further, women who expect to receive love after sex are viewed as stupid because after understanding the game, and agreeing to play it through acquiescence, they have no rights to demand or expect anything at all; not even a guilt, or sympathy, phone call after. Many young women today, hook up after being pursued because they've posted a half naked Instagram photo of themselves. They then cry and walk around anxiously dying inside, while pretending on the outside to be OK with being dissed, de-valued, and spit out like trash, when the guy doesn't call again. Or worse, he only calls when he wants to trample on your self worth once more.

My college aged niece, who attends UCLA, shares countless stories of completely self-inflicted sexual and mental abuse, by her girlfriends on themselves, for participating in this obviously destructive pattern of female spiritual genocide. While grateful she herself possesses the prerequisite spiritual maturity to understand the game clearly, I am saddened constantly that so many young women today do not.

They allow the bar to remain so low there isn't a scumbag alive who can't get under it. I say this with a heart that would love to see these misguided and misinformed men, who desire to slide in under these lowered bars of self esteem, all be saved and spirit filled. However, for every game we seem to establish in the world there are always players willing to play it. And, this is where women have caused their own self-fulfilling prophecies of pain, rejection, and disrespect. Girls, you have nobody to blame but yourselves. I played this game once also. It eventually turns on you and plays you.   Why?

Identity check!!!! Because YOU ARE A DAUGHTER OF THE KING!

In reality, God HIMSELF created us to *love* us. Why on earth would He want us giving ourselves to anyone, or anything, that doesn't love us with the same honor and respect that He Himself has for us?! We will never find comfort and peace in selling ourselves for far less than we inherently know we are worth.

Jesus commands us to love one another. If we loved one another we would not want to mess with each other, unless and until we stepped into full marriage commitment, which is ultimately what each of us deserves, as determined by God, not me.

Girls intuitively know they deserve a guy to love them after sex. Guys know intuitively that they should treat girls a certain way after sex. Yet, we are taught socially that these expectations and strings are not a part of things because 'sex is not love.'

Well, here is the final and absolute truth; sex *is* love. It is the highest expression of love. It is the ultimate act of love. We more than lie to ourselves, and to each other, when we say that sex is possible without expectations or strings attached. Inherent in our human design is the need for expectations and strings, once we've given the sum total of ourselves, i.e. our love, to someone sexually.

Therefore a man shall leave his father and mother and be joined to his wife, and they shall become one flesh.
Genesis 2:24 (NKJV)

How can you not have expectations and strings when you've become one flesh with someone? You can't. Therefore, the safest place for expectations and strings is within the ultimate place where expectations and strings are embraced and celebrated; marriage. The safest place for sex is marriage. Love should cause you to desire marriage and sex. Period. Every other twisting and manipulating of this truth causes horrendous results to you and to the world.

Trust me. If you don't fully believe this as you read it now you will see that God was right in the way He built things to work for us. Even if you can walk away free of emotions and expectations from situations a few times, the fact that you're walking away empty handed repeatedly will begin to take a toll on your heart, your soul, and your mind. Your entire life will eventually reflect the consequences of sexual abuse, which is what this behavior is. Whether at your own hands, or someone else's hands, it's still sexual abuse. It doesn't matter, in the end, who's empowered to be the one abusing you; it only matters that you're being abused.

Ultimately, the lifestyle we are calling normal and accepted in the world today will crush us one heart, and one life, at a time. Eventually, you too will understand that you have been deceived and are in fact deceiving others. If you are involved in mindsets that you recognize as you're reading, perhaps, the game you're playing, even unknowingly, has in fact already begun to play you. Soon you'll realize, that all along, the war that has been waged against the God given truth that we were created for love, marriage partnership, and family, has robbed years from your life, and threatens to leave you empty handed at the finish line, feeling like much less than you were created to feel.

Thankfully, God had, and still has, a plan. No perversion or twisting of God's original plans for us will ever turn out to be good and healthy in the long run. Eventually, the long run turns quite simply into a long, long, run. And, when you're exhausted, and you will eventually be exhausted, you will have to face the harsh realities of truth. There are consequences to believing the lies of the enemy. I would suggest you wake up and seek the truth because the truth is found in the Word of God and that truth really will set you free!

But, on that night, back then, like many in the world today, I was still in bondage to the lies. The lies of this world were my truth and all forms of the media diet I consumed and the environment that I lived in reinforced those lies.

Needless to say, when the door to his apartment opened I followed Miloj inside believing that I would surely feel better, and possibly get back at River some more for not meeting my expectations, and for not understanding the strings that were attached to my love.

Why do we girls think we punish a guy by having sex with another one?

It wasn't even about this handsome, European, stranger that said all the right things at the bar all night. It was about River, and every single thing that had happened to me in my childhood and throughout my youth. How many times do we exact payment on a bill created by someone else? And, how many times, do we step into major danger by turning to things outside of God for answers, comfort, and victory?

I am certain tears from heaven fall, as His relentless pursuit of His kids has no limits or places He won't go to reclaim what belongs to Him.

If I ascend up into heaven, thou art there: if I make my bed in hell, behold, thou art there
Psalm 139:8

14

THE LIE BECOMES THE TRUTH

But mark this: There will be terrible times in the last days. People will be lovers of themselves, lovers of money, boastful, proud, abusive, disobedient to their parents, ungrateful, unholy, without love, unforgiving, slanderous, without self-control, brutal, not lovers of the good, treacherous, rash, conceited, lovers of pleasure rather than lovers of God— having a form of godliness but denying its power. Have nothing to do with such people.
They are the kind who worm their way into homes and gain control over gullible women, who are loaded down with sins and are swayed by all kinds of evil desires, always learning but never able to come to a knowledge of the truth. Just as Jannes and Jambres opposed Moses, so also these teachers oppose the truth. They are men of depraved minds, who, as far as the faith is concerned, are rejected. But they will not get very far because, as in the case of those men, their folly will be clear to everyone.
2 Timothy 3:1-9 (NIV)

The next few weeks with Miloj were a blur of sex and questions with answers that made no sense. I paid zero attention to the fact that none of his stories seemed to add up to any possible truth. He told me he was a model and well known in Europe. He showed me modeling cards with him as the face of Armani and Ferre, but I always expected they were in some way fake. I didn't really know who he was, where he was from, how he made money, or why he was apparently being evicted from his apartment. Down inside I don't think I really even cared. He was a distraction from my career which seemed stalled, my heart which was broken in a million pieces, and my life which was a secret blur of coke filled days to numb the pain and silence the voices in my head constantly reminding me of how miserable and confused and lost I was.

I was smitten with Miloj's looks, satisfied by him physically, and distracted by his constant presence and the attention that he provided me. Since, he couldn't fill the real void, I kept silent about my daily habit and my circle of one famous actor, two playboy playmates, and a cast of characters whose names I didn't even know that would stop by to drop off whatever I wanted when supplies ran low. These were my hidden 'drug friends' that I didn't dare bring around Lenny or anyone who REALLY loved me. You may have friends like this yourself to one degree or another. They're the friends with whom you do things that you wouldn't want anybody who really loves you, or wants you to be well in your life, would approve of or do. These are the friends that you know are only there for a short season because you don't want to make a lifestyle of what you do with them. These friends you hide from your real friends completely.

"Baby, do you have any friends who like cocaine?" he asked curiously.
"WHAT!" I replied shocked.
"Do you have any friends who use cocaine?" he repeated with a deadpan stare.
"No, of course not!!!" I lied emphatically. A long pause followed.
"Good, because girls here all use cocaine and I don't want woman who use drugs or woman with friends who use drugs." He stared through me. Was he happy or disappointed in my answer?

In hindsight, the morning after we first met and slept together, I wish I were clear enough when he asked me this question to see that what registered, when I answered him, was disappointment.

I lied to his face not wanting him to know I was using it and I had friends who were too. Why? Because, I knew it was wrong and that this state of abuse was temporary for me. I knew somehow that I didn't want to add to what I knew was a problem but I wanted a way out of the problematic behavior. I chose to see his question as one filled with hope and promise that he was a man desirous of a good girl to live a good life. I chose to see his question and his response as evidence that I could go forward with him and find a way out of the madness I was engaged in. A guy who wanted a good girl. That's what I wanted because that's what I was; a good girl trapped in a world of sin related to pain and pain related to sin.

The next month we were inseparable. I began to pull back on the drug and alcohol filled nights and get clearer about wanting to change my life for the better. Miloj was a welcome distraction because in all honesty I wasn't working, my mom was supporting me, and I felt like I was in a life holding pattern. However, just as things were looking up Miloj threw me a major curve ball and told me that he had to leave for Paris to work for a couple weeks. I was fine with the break from my instant relationship with him but I wasn't fine with his statement two weeks after he had left California and returned to Paris.

"I don't feel to come back unless you marry me."
"MARRY YOU! Miloj, what do you mean? We've known each other a month. And, you told me you were just going to Paris to work for a couple weeks and then coming back to LA?!"
"LA is not for me. I don't want to live like a dog. I hate Americans. I am man who needs to live here. I work in Paris. I get respect here."
"But, you said you were coming back. What about...us?" I questioned.
"I don't feel to have *us* unless you marry me and *prove* you love me."
He hung up the phone in my face. I was speechless and in a daze from our phone call.

The next couple days passed in a self-induced mind numbing haze. I didn't know what to do so I continued what I had been doing in even greater quantities than before I met Miloj. The up, the down, the lack of sleep, was all overwhelming me. I couldn't run far enough fast enough. He was supposed to come back. Now he was saying he wouldn't unless I married him. This seemed completely ridiculous and extreme. But, I reasoned, what was marriage anyway? It's not like I knew anybody who had ever really had a good one, besides River's parents, I thought to myself. I would just do it and if it didn't work out I would divorce him and move on. I called him in Paris with my decision to relent to his wishes.

"Well, can we do it here so my mom and my family can be with me?"
"No, I want you to come alone." He stated matter of factly.
"Alone! Miloj, why? It's my wedding?!"
He slammed his phone down in my face, leaving me sitting speechless again. Hours passed and then he called back a different man.

"OK my love but you come here and we do it in Paris. You bring them here. Paris is so beautiful. They will love it. Let's do it here." Go to Paris? He was making a convincing and romantic case for Paris, and I was tired of fighting. I was battling all day, every day, inside with my own unexplained pain and confusion. I didn't need to battle with him. "Well, that could be nice I guess." I silently reflected on details. "So I need to organize things with my mom and my friends. Airplane travel and hotels." Excitement started to settle in.
"You think to much for them. No, I change my mind! I don't want to do it. You are not type of wife for me" Once again he slammed down the phone. Another day or two would pass.

"Miloj, I've been calling and calling. Please stop acting so crazy. I do love you but..." But, you're making me crazy! But, I don't know you. But you don't know me. But I don't even know myself. The thoughts behind the 'but' were numerous, complicated, and incredible. He would remain quiet and let me squirm, cry, and beg, while I frustratedly cycled through emotions that I couldn't handle.

This behavior went on repeatedly for two months.

He grew increasingly short tempered. There was a very dark, cruel, side that began surfacing in the two months we would spend navigating this whole marriage in Paris and who would be allowed by him to attend.

"Miloj, you didn't return my call yesterday. Please don't disappear on me." I became the girl I never liked in the movie. Needy. Desperate. Weak. Broken and lacking dignity. I was losing whatever self-respect I had even pretended for years to have.
"I want to marry you but I *need* to have my mom and some family there to be with me. Lenny will be in Europe to. I can ask him to give me away." A question that went over, a couple weeks later, like a brick to Lenny's head.

My brother, and close friend, thought that these escapades with Miloj would have ended quickly, or at least as soon as he left the country after the first few weeks. He didn't realize the depth of my despair and the trouble I was really in yet. He did realize he hated the guy though.

"There's something about him that's off girl. He's not for you. You sure you wanna marry him? C'mon, wake up." Lenny stated convinced. I wasn't sure at all that I wanted to marry him. But I had to do something positive about my current mess of a life. This would be a fresh start I reasoned with myself.

"I don't care about Lenny. He thinks he is better than me." Miloj stated arrogantly. Yet another man jealous of my brother was all I could think to myself.
"No, he doesn't. He's not like that. At all." I retorted.

It was actually Miloj who was nasty and condescending to people. Lenny, on the other hand was a sweetheart.

"I want woman who is sure...woman who would do anything for only me."

With that he hung up the phone in my face. Again. This is how the next few conversations went. They got crazier and crazier as his control of me became more and more mental. I felt as if I was literally losing my mind. I was under an emotional siege caused by the turmoil he kept throwing me into with each tense, angry, manipulative phone call. With each conversation I lost a little more of whatever dignity I had left, and I became a bit more desperate not to lose...yet again.

Each time the phone slammed, the tears fell, or he teased me back into his web, I responded by inhaling more confusion from a plate of white powder, sleeping less and less, all in an effort to deal with Miloj's new rounds of abuse and criticism; which were now quite personal.

"You're fat."

"Miloj, I barely eat at all."   With all the cocaine I was using the last couple months I actually never ate. I lived on alcohol to come down and blow to get back up. Food wasn't really part of my life equation and at 5'10 I was barely 119 pounds.

"Wife for me cannot be fat. Ugly. I am important man here. I need important wife."

"Lenny said he would give me away." I sighed.

"He should. You are his sister. He should honor me."

Honor YOU was all I could think. Why on earth should YOU be honored!? WHO ARE YOU?! The words screamed in my head but I couldn't dare let them come out my mouth. I was trying to hang on to the marriage plans everyone was excitedly making around us. He sniffed in disgust and hung up the phone. There was never a goodbye. Silence was the sign he had hung up and moved on. I sighed, actually relieved whenever we got off the phone without calling the wedding off for the 25th time that week alone.

Lenny left to go on tour, which left me alone in a world of chaos and noise, amidst the silence and loneliness of not only my apartment, but also my life. I truly didn't know what to do about anything. I wasn't getting any career breaks in just under a year and a half out of law school. I was relying on my mom financially and she wanted it to stop. My actor friend, whom I loved but knew was walking on the edge, suggested casually one day that we try something more fun, like heroine.
"Are you nuts?!" I said. This was a complete non-negotiable for me even in my temporary insanity! I began to get afraid of this whole life of casual drug use.

I was completely torn and distraught over how to keep Miloj happy. We lived in a complete state of volatility. My response to it was to numb my mind and heart. I simply couldn't handle anymore pain. I was on emotional overload. What started out as casual cocaine use which I thought said 'oh look how on the edge I'm living with my famous friends,' within six months, became a habit I was using to escape dealing with any of my issues whatsoever.

One night at about two-o-clock in the morning I was especially filled with fear and anxiety. I was hurting deeply inside and needed to get out of my body. And, if I had to remain trapped inside of myself I needed to kill everything inside. I had to turn off the pain and the hurt. Lenny was gone on tour. Miloj was in Paris manipulating my mind even when we weren't on the phone. My mother couldn't bare a conversation with me because I was so erratic and all over the place. I wanted to explain what I was doing, and that I needed help, but I was so afraid to tell her and disappoint her even more in me. I was her golden child, nearly one year out of law school, unemployed by choice because I was pursuing a career in Hollywood. It all seemed like such a waste of talent, money, and brains to her.

I made a call and within minutes a guy showed up at my front door. He came in to sit with me so I could sample what I was buying from him. He was really unsavory looking and I had a check in my spirit about letting him in my apartment with me alone at nearly three-o-clock in the morning. I asked myself what I was thinking and doing, but I wanted what he had, and I didn't want to be rude and now shut the door in his face. I was such a people pleaser. I prayed to God that He would keep me safe.

He sat and went about his business lining things up. I remember, with complete clarity, bending down to do the two lines on the table. When I looked up, it was no longer the creepy guy who walked in my apartment, but he had morphed into a demon. An actual demon was sitting in front of me. I will NEVER forget it. His physical face changed completely, right at my kitchen table, where I had invited him into my life.

I stared at the demon in front of me speechless. He smiled. A knowing smile. A smile that said I've got you and I win. It knew he was destroying me. I understood that I was looking in the face of a spirit that literally hated me and was enjoying the torture I was putting myself, and God, through. I was so terrified that I quickly paid him and suggested he leave. As I shut the door behind him I walked in circles for hours and hours, in my apartment, in fear. I thought that no matter how bad this marriage situation could get it couldn't get any worse than where I was in that apartment on that night.

Or could it?!

My sister drove my mom and my aunt and I to the airport in Los Angeles to catch our late night departure for Paris. My mom was in heaven. This was a dream come true for her. Her daughter was marrying a gorgeous, European, man in Paris. She was soon going to be free of the stress and turmoil I had become in my not so silent cry for help. A cry that nobody, not even her, heard. I wish she had. I certainly provided enough clues.

"Cynthia, do you really wanna do this? Mom you're tripping. Don't make her do this."
"I'm not making her do anything." My mother stated.
"She shouldn't do this. Something feels off to me. You've known this guy three months. I'm just sayin..."
My younger sister, Sheila, born with an abundance of street smarts and common sense, was beside herself with worry and objection to me running off to Paris to marry a man I had know three months, two of which had been on the phone. She also recognized that I was out of control and couldn't understand why nobody was calling me on it.

"I like him. He believes in marriage. There's nothing wrong with that." My mother retorted. He had thoroughly charmed her and she didn't see the dark side I had lived with the last couple months on the phone. How would she have? He would only ever show that side to me.

They discussed me as if I wasn't there. I felt like a cat on a hot tin roof the whole way to the airport. They tried to ask why I seemed so anxious and kept crying and I told them I was fine. Actually, I was to wired to even think straight enough to explain that I didn't know what I was feeling, but that this was probably a huge mistake, because I had no clue what it meant to get married, nor did I even want to *be* married.

At moments growing up I though that I wanted a baby. I just never wanted a husband. Since I wouldn't have a baby without being married I never knew how the baby thing would happen. Marriage was a foreign concept to me. A concept I was only ever open to trying with

River and that turned out to be a disaster from which I clearly still hadn't recovered.

As we boarded the plane I excused myself to go to the bathroom prior to take off. My mother was annoyed with me because I was acting erratic. The crying. The constant drama. The outbursts. The constant trips to the bathroom to feed the void. She was over me and I don't blame her one bit.

I locked the door inside the small bathroom on board the plane and emptied out a large pile of white powder and snorted all of it. I stood there stunned. I should have been shocked that I boarded a plane with drugs and then finished them off literally in the business class bathroom. But, I was way beyond shocking myself, after the last six months of self inflicted drama like I've never been in before or since.

I returned to my seat, quickly polished off two glasses of wine, and resolved myself to my fate. The fake face I put on said 'wow I'm getting married in Paris.' Eventually, I laid back in a stupor to try and sleep, while my mom and my aunt giggled and chatted excited to be flying to France for my wedding. As usual, I was providing a glamorously good time for all parties involved and invited.

My life, to everyone else, seemed like a fairytale; gorgeous man with an accent who loved me and wanted to marry me. In Paris!

I was miserable.

15

SHE WHO FINDS A HUSBAND

However, let each one of you love his wife as himself, and let the wife see that she respects her husband.
Ephesians 5:33 (ESV)

Together for ten years, and married for six, at the time of writing this book, I am still no expert on marriage. It's the hardest thing I've ever done in my life because of the many mindsets that God has had to reveal and transform. Getting to the alter was a road filled with confronting demons, inner healing, and surrender on levels I've never experienced before in my life. I had to find and marry ME, before I would ever find and marry the man who became my husband, my real husband; the one God audibly spoke to me about.

I know this much for certain. A man cannot love his wife as himself if he first doesn't love God fully. And, a woman cannot respect her husband if she doesn't respect God; who teaches her how to respect herself.

Roger and I met, oddly enough, on an airplane about sixteen years after the fateful flight I was on that day with my mother and aunt. It would be a very different kind of meeting. I had long since surrendered to the call on my life and wanted nothing and no one except Jesus. I didn't even want my career in the same way anymore. I wanted more of Him, more understanding of Him, more knowledge and revelation of Him, more of Him in me and through me. I was all in for Him. Jesus had proven Himself to me and I had done it my way long enough to know that He was right and I was capable of only making messes without Him.

By the time I met Roger, I wanted to walk in the power of whatever my God given, God created, destiny was. I trusted that whatever it was, no matter how high or low, no matter how rich or poor, I wanted to be a washed clean Bride of Christ. I wanted to pursue that on a deeper level, even though I didn't really know how, and even though my life still looked more worldly than it would by the time Roger and I would marry four years later.

My husband is a natural born teacher. He raised four sons in his first marriage; a marriage he fought twenty six years to make work but could never win the battle in their one sided war. On the day we met, I was headed to QVC to do a product presentation for a line of inspirational jewelry I was designing called Love Conquers All. I was not attracted to him at all. No bells rang and no sirens screeched. My usual lustful, emotional, pre-requisites for love were long since set aside as traps and snares to be dealt with even though I wasn't completely sure how they would be dealt with and defeated forever.

I was seeking God fully. A month prior to meeting Roger, God had given me a vision of myself as a bridge stretched between the secular world and the Kingdom and He showed me people walking literally across my body and into the Kingdom. It was so powerful. I desired only that this vision would become a reality someday. I was committed to dying to myself, and to all that I knew, in order to live for Christ. Again, I didn't fully comprehend all that this choice meant back then, but since my flesh wasn't running the show, God was able to be fully present between Roger and I from our first hello. This fact alone enabled us to build a strong enough foundation to one day become husband and wife.

"So, do you read that thing?" He asked. He was referring to the Bible on my lap. I had boarded my flight after crying in the lounge for an hour because of something a friend said and because I was simply convinced, once again, that God *had* to be exhausted with me because I sure was. My spirit was just tired. I was over everything; my career, people, and my own inner struggles which seemed to have returned although in a much more grounded way than in my twenties. I felt as if I must be to blame for this wilderness I felt I was in, in my life, and I wasn't sure what to do next; except lean on Him for answers and help. So, I intended to spend the entire flight in the Bible reading and seeking God in prayer. I had achieved at least this much spiritual maturity by this flight .

Do you read that thing?" He asked again. Great I figured he was the unbelieving type who was less tolerant than they say we Christians are and now he was going to tease me or make a rude comment.

"Yes, I read this thing?" I glared at him and rolled my eyes now noticing his wedding ring and thinking to myself, "Really God, I have finally sworn off married men, and I'm working at swearing off sex, and all I get hit on by are married men who want sex?!" Give me a break I pleaded with God thinking surely this guy is going to hell for hitting on me in Jesus' name.

Then he leaned across the aisle and mumbled a scripture verse to me. "What?" I said surprised that he knew scripture.
"Read it. I think it's for you." He leaned back in his seat as the plane took off and he closed his eyes to sleep. In the years to come I would learn that he was silently listening in prayer to what God might want to say through him.

I opened my Bible to the verse he had given me and read it while not wanting him to have the satisfaction of knowing I was checking it out. I was immediately smacked in the gut. The verse spoke exactly to what

I had asked the Lord for revelation about earlier in the day. I had asked God for revelation about fear.

For the first time in my life I was battling fear in ways I had never experienced. Fear in a paralyzing way. Fear of everything. Fear of living. Fear of dying. Fear of being unworthy of God's love. Fear of flying. Fear this man was hitting on me. Fear. And, the scripture I was now reading, given to me by this stranger, that I feared was hitting on me, was speaking into the very core of the *'come to Jesus'* meeting I had boarded the plane intending to have with Him in His Word.

For God did not give us a spirit of fear, but of power, love, and a sound mind.
2 Timothy 1:7

Some translations of this verse read 'self control,' some read 'self discipline.' Whatever the case, I couldn't believe that this man had given me a verse that was clearly a revelation from God to me.

I began to question whether my vanity was driving this whole encounter too much. Maybe, just maybe, he wasn't hitting on me?! Maybe this was a Divine appointment as I called them?! I know from much experience that God has placed, and will place, angels, or people, or events, in our path to give us a word or instruction from Him at moments when we need to hear from Him the most. I needed to hear from Him, on that day, badly. I had spent an hour and a half in the first class lounge, prior to boarding the flight, hiding tears behind my black sunglasses and floppy black hat. I sat contemplating not just the scripture, but what the mans motives were for giving it to me. Then, as if he read my thoughts, he looked over at me, opened his briefcase, and took out a Bible.
"I wasn't hitting on you." He stated flatly. "I'm married. It's just that I read it too." With that he held up his Bible.

I almost laughed out loud with relief. The last thing I needed, wanted, or desired, was a married man. I had been there, and done that. All I wanted was Jesus. If this guy could help me get more of that then we could talk.

And boy did we. We ended up talking through a five hour Bible study on the plane from LAX to Philadelphia. His employee, Andy, changed seats with me so I could be seated next to Roger to hear better his teaching. Andy had a slight smile on his face as we crossed in the aisle. He had clearly witnessed these moments many, many, times. I would one day tell others that my husband has an airplane ministry. If you sit next to him at 30,000 feet you're gonna get saved! Period. More folks have encountered Jesus through my husband on airplanes than in most churches! Thank God he travels ALL the time. I think God gives him supernatural stamina with his crazy travel schedule because he is so valuable to the Kingdom on a plane.

I wouldn't know for many months that he was actually separated for quite some time and divorcing when we met. Our connection was not physical in any way. We only remained in contact because he felt lead to introduce me to a friend of his named Brad Dacus. Brad is a lovely man who runs an amazing organization that fights for the rights of Christians to be Christians and express their faith today. I am an attorney by education, having graduated USC Law School, and I was fully immersed in Hollywood. There fore, Roger thought I could be of great use on the board of The Pacific Justice League, Brad's organization. I also desperately wanted to continue gleaning Rogers's advice about raising my, then fourteen year old, son. I was terrified that I had dropped the ball on a couple key prophecies spoken over him as an infant, and let him get to imprinted by the worlds point of view in the west side private schools he went to, where 'God' was a nice word people sometimes used. He had no real faith. Money, self, fame, and rejection were far more current conditions that I was concerned he needed some grounding to deal with. The enemy had launched all out attack on my child from day one.

I recognized immediately that Roger could teach me some things spiritually about the Lord, and how to get my son on track, and surrendered, to a Jesus he had never seen me fully surrendered to in any real way before now. I was in damage control mode and I saw that perhaps, Roger, could help.

I worked hard to make Roger my friend and to always invite his wife along to pray with us, or to visit me, at work events with his kids. She never came. He was usually rather vague about her absence, and their marriage, so I respected his privacy. I was, selfishly, happy he was married because I didn't want any complications that could arise if he were attracted to me on any level. I wanted, and needed, a friend who knew Christ. Since I had always been a guy's girl I was quite accustomed to having guy friends. He was, however, my first guy friend who was really a man of God, rooted and grounded in the Word, with a depth of revelation and understanding that I had *never* encountered. It was, and still is, amazing.

I was growing by leaps and bounds daily because of him. I had so many questions about the next level of my faith walk that I wanted answered. I craved the information he was able to provide, even though he often rebuked me like a big brother for some of what he called my very worldly mindsets. Most of those mindsets still had to do with men, and wouldn't be undone prior to inner healing, since they were deeply rooted in a lot of brokenness. More on that later.

I was dating a man I had known for many years, in my career life, that I reconnected with days after the weekend Roger and I met on the plane. He was an older, Jewish, man who had once run Disney, with Michael Eisner, and for whom I had worked, when I was younger, on a daytime talk show with Terry Bradshaw. I had always had a bit of a crush on him so when we reconnected, and he was newly divorced, we began dating. He was such a comfort and encouragement to me, even in my new attempts at a higher level of spiritual surrender. While, I don't think he completely understood my faith, he did respect it, and I felt admired for my convictions. He encouraged and supported me greatly as a woman, and a creatively talented person, which was really healing for me back then. I was realizing, however, that being unequally yoked spiritually really hinders the work of plowing a Kingdom field, so to speak. Roger would often help me sort through my growing awareness with answers that were solely rooted in the word of God. I really wasn't interested in the opinions of men at this point in my life. All I could hear, or wanted to hear, was the voice of God. Roger helped me navigate my way to a deeper level of hearing Him and our friendship was supporting my efforts to root solidly in all that He had to say.

"Hey you busy?" I was driving up Coldwater Canyon toward Mulholland.
"Uh, I have a minute. What's up?" Roger replied.
"I just wanted to pray through some stuff." I answered
"OK." He said.
As we prayed, about my son, I then had an odd sense to also pray for him and his wife and for clarity and peace about their home.
"Ummm, Why did you pray that?" He asked when we finished.
"Pray what?" I had prayed as a leading but I really hadn't thought much about it.
"About me and my wife and clarity in my home?" Roger asked.
"I don't know. I just felt lead too." I didn't know what else to say.
He was silent a few moments past awkward.
"I think I should tell you something. My wife and I are separated and divorcing and we have been since before we met."
"What? Wow. You are?! But you wear a wedding ring! Why didn't you ever tell me?" I asked surprised.

"I wear my wedding ring because I haven't really felt release from the Lord to date and I never told you because, no offense, but it's not your business for me to discuss my wife, and our marriage, with you. It's not appropriate."

"WHOA! OK!" I said out loud. " A man who doesn't feel compelled to throw his ex under a bus in Los Angeles? Now, THIS, is a miracle!" All I could do was laugh with respect and admiration. "Well, don't start liking me now that you're single, and mess up our friendship, or I will kill you!" I was laughing but also completely serious. I didn't want things to get weird. He was so important to me as a friend. Spiritually he was a lifeline and had become my best friend. I played no roles with him as I always had with men. Absent sex as a driving force I felt free to just be myself. I didn't feel the need to lobby for anything or sell my greatness in any way. All I had to give was my real, honest, friendship, which was possible because he wasn't my goal, in any way, as men had often been in the past. It felt great to have the freedom to just 'be' in the relationship and grow as two people with a deep and common faith as their mutual bond in life.

Jesus as the springboard for our friendship, absent any fleshly desires taking the lead, set the foundation for our entire marriage. I was so in love with Jesus and focused on Him that I was literally blindsided when God spoke to me audibly telling me Roger was my husband. The restoration and healing that have come have been miraculous because he was not my goal; God was. Only because we allowed God to have His way with us, keeping our eyes narrowly on Him, and blindly following Him, have we been blessed with the ultimate union. We followed Him all the way to a stretch of white sandy beach on the island of Virgin Gorda, where four years after we met, before our closest family, and just a few friends, we got married.

In those years, I would confront my childhood brokenness and go through an amazing and transformative inner healing process. But, it has been an understanding of the marriage paradigm, as set forth in the scripture below, which enabled me to understand a marriage relationship as something amazing, that I was created for in the first place.

Wives, submit yourselves to your own husbands as you do to the Lord. For the husband is the head of the wife as Christ is the head of the church, his body, of which he is the Savior. Now as the church submits to Christ, so also wives should submit to their husbands in everything. Husbands, love your wives, just as Christ loved the church and gave himself up for her to make her holy, cleansing her by the washing with water through the word, and to present her to himself as a radiant church, without stain or wrinkle or any other blemish, but holy and blameless. In this same way, husbands ought to love their wives as their own bodies. He who loves his wife loves himself. After all, no one ever hated their own body, but they feed and care for their body, just as Christ does the church— for we are members of his body. "For this reason a man will leave his father and mother and be united to his wife, and the two will become one flesh." This is a profound mystery— but I am talking about Christ and the church. However, each one of you also must love his wife as he loves himself, and the wife must respect her husband.
Ephesians 5:22-33 (NIV)

Many people misuse this passage and misrepresent it as suppressing women. They love to say that telling wives to submit to their husbands is a negative. They speak incorrectly and with such passion. This passage is all about our relationship with Jesus. It's about what it means to be the Bride of Christ. You would have to take time to know Him to understand. Sadly, the loudest voices against Jesus are from those who have no knowledge of Him at all. They've rarely, if ever, even read the Bible in a way that is evidence of truly seeking knowledge of Him. If they had they would find that it is very, very, easy to submit to Jesus. He loved us enough to die for us. He loved me enough to die for me and He loves *you* enough that He died for you even though you may not know or understand it, yet.

In this same way, earthly marriage should look the same. Knowing that my husband loves me enough to die for me makes it easy to submit to him when he feels strongly lead by God in a decision or an action. And since he loves me enough to die for me he would never abuse his power and lord over me like some crazed, sexist, egomaniac. Ladies those are not the men God tells you to marry. Get in line with Him, and follow Him, and He will lead you correctly in every way; including to your husband.

16

PARIS

"My people are destroyed from lack of knowledge. Because you have rejected knowledge, I also reject you as my priests; because you have ignored the law of your God, I also will ignore your children."
Hosea 4:6-7 (NIV)

Paris was a nightmare in the natural; a perfect storm in the supernatural.

According to Hosea 4:6, we, God's people, are destroyed because we reject knowledge. Our refusal to pursue relationship with God, and to allow Him to teach us through the example of His love, leaves us open to trying to fill voids in our lives through other means. Hosea calls this choice idolatry (false relationship with false gods) and warns us about falling victim to the "spirit of prostitution" discussed in that same chapter. Tired of waiting, we find ourselves clinging to whatever crosses our paths; sex, drugs, fame, money, men, women. Content to have something, anything, to occupy our time, and someone, anyone, to talk to, and make us 'feel' some kind of way, we make gods of other things instead of following God to the exclusion of everything.

If we pursued the knowledge God provides by being in a relationship with Him, and if we got to know Him through His Word, which explains everything about how we should live and think, we would avoid many heartaches, trials, and tribulations. If we humans would only stop rejecting the knowledge of God we would see a complete change in our world. Yet, we avoid Him. We choose distraction. We choose to limp along, delayed by all kinds of things, over a sure swift victory in all the areas of our life that require us to use Godly knowledge to overcome and stay clear of a great many problems.

As we left Charles De Gaulle airport with Miloj, my choices back then were evident. They were rooted, as are most people's, in the options I felt I had to choose from.

We were all excitedly surveying Paris. I was excitedly pointing out the Eiffel Tower to my mom and aunt. Miloj was polite and distant. He seemed lost in a world of thought. I had slept soundly on the flight, exhausted from my own three months of total chaos. Now, however, awake and well rested, I reflected on the promise I made to myself to never do drugs again when I finished the last bit of white powder in the bathroom on the plane. I felt strangely alive and happy for the first time in months. Hope began to fill me again and the promise of a clean, new, future brought a bright smile to my face and joy to my heart. I was determined in that moment to make this marriage work. I knew I could do it. I felt blessed by God to be in Paris and looked forward to fun times and a new chapter.

I was determined to give this marriage a try. I needed to start over, to be free from my drug buddies, and the cast of characters I had been around the past few months. I had family and friends in Paris to celebrate with me, and support me, and I needed to try and enjoy this new life. I stared at the man driving the car, who in all honesty, I barely knew. He was my new start. Miloj was my savior, I thought to myself, as we were driving into Paris. I smiled reflectively at him. He shifted awkwardly in return.

Within hours, I realized the fantasy I was constructing in my head was nothing like the reality I was now presented with.

We dropped my mom, and my aunt, off at the gorgeous little boutique hotel off Avenue Montagne that they had chosen, before driving to the place Miloj had taken for us, in St. Germain Du Pres.

He silently showed me around the little one bedroom apartment. It was perfect for young lovers. It had a small bathroom and kitchen but a nice sized bedroom and living room with large windows that looked out onto the wonderful little street below.

"It's great, Miloj." I cooed.

I unpacked as he watched. It felt as if he wanted to say something. But he didn't. I noticed that he had a horrible cold. He was sniffling constantly and needed to retreat often to the bathroom to get tissue to blow his nose. It was a bit chilly in Paris in November so I understood how he could be a bit sick.

I went in the kitchen to make us some tea. While the teapot boiled I changed clothes. I figured we could get in bed and rest. It was evening and I felt we needed some alone time to reconnect and find each other again. We didn't share much beyond the physical so that was the only go-to I had. I knew there I had mastered the art of seduction and I was in a hurry to get some control back.

When I returned from the kitchen he said coldly.

"I'm going out. Put some clothes on."

"Miloj, we just got here. Can't we stay in and talk and be together." I moved closer to him.

He pushed me away firmly and said, "You need to learn to be wife for me then maybe I give you sex."

" What?!" I blurted out incredulously. He looked at me and walked out of the room.

"Get dressed." This was the beginning of the withholding and manipulating of sex with me to control and punish me when he felt I needed it. Since this was the only glue we had between us, the reality that we were total strangers would become bigger and bigger.

What followed was the torturous education in what it meant to him to be his wife. He was to be given total control. He was to never be questioned. I was to do whatever he said even if it was criminal. I would wear what he wanted, when he wanted it, and he would use everything and every person around me in whatever way served his desires and interests. I, in turn, would follow him around, now desperate to make him love me and want me again; as if he ever did. Nothing I did was good enough and he talked to me worse than a dog. He had names for referring to me and addressing me regularly; Bitch. Pig. Stupid American. Fat bitch. Fat pig. I was incapable in his estimations of being the woman he *deserved* for a wife.

He hissed insults at me twenty-two out of twenty-four hours a day. At 115 pounds my 5'10" frame was skeletal, yet he referred to me constantly as fat, telling me I needed to never eat. As the last drops of self-esteem were squeezed from my corpse I no longer felt human. A rollercoaster of emotional abuse and destruction began within mere hours of my arrival in Paris and it would only get worse before it got better. Luckily, I had no drugs to rely on to escape my reeling emotions now. I would have to deal in some way.

We went out until four or five a.m. nearly every night with a cast of 'friends' of his who all hung out in the hip places in Paris like the famed, Le Bain Douche, and expected VIP treatment. I didn't know any of them. Yet, they all seemed like losers. There were two Italian brothers who seemed to have money, and more class, however, than everyone else who showed up after the first few days. They were more educated and refined than Miloj. Of the crew of constant people, I liked them best, although I was clueless as to who they were. They were, at least, kind to me as the chaos and spiral of the following days in Paris unfolded.

There was also a famous model, named Katoucha. She was tall, super thin, and elegant. She, too, made an effort to be kind to me realizing I was in way over my head with Miloj. On one particularly cruel night, Miloj twisted my arm behind my back in a dark hallway of Bain Douche, and threatened to break it, because Lenny dishonored him by coming late to meet us at what I thought was my wedding dinner. As it turned out, Miloj had traded the whole night of drinks and food for his friends on Lenny's name and the club had printed up invites that read Miloj presents Lenny Kravitz. When I realized he had used not just me, but my brother, to promote himself and feed his friends, I wanted to kill him. When I confronted him he tried to break my arm for defending Lenny who was simply late coming from work. Katoucha, found me crying in the ladies room after the incident and held me trying to console me. I realized that I had made a huge mistake and I was now desperate to save face and make it work. She had such a deep understanding of the fact that I was a child in over my head and she just held me as I cried saying over and over in her broken English, "You are just baby. I promise it will be OK. You must be woman now. But you are still just baby."

No matter how much I protested about going out night after night, dragging my mom and my aunt and my best girlfriend, Lisa, and her husband, Keith, along behind us, Miloj didn't care. The night was his world. He slept most of the day and then had meetings in the afternoons with various men, for whom I was always told to leave the room. They always spoke in other languages.
"Miloj, I had no idea you spoke so many languages." I said one afternoon.
"I am European. What do you think? You stupid, American,......!! And why do you have that in your hair?" He asked disgustedly.
"What?"
"That! It's wet." He pointed to my ponytail holder.
"Miloj, it's raining outside all day of course it's wet."
"Take it out! It stinks!" With that he struck me and I flew across the room.

For the next couple hours I cried on my moms shoulder. Both she and my aunt, and Keith and Lisa, decided enough was enough. I was leaving. My suitcase was already packed because Miloj had taken all the clothes I brought and threw them in a suitcase to send back to America with my mom. I arrived to a closet full of new clothes and shoes he had bought me to replace all my things. This would have been romantic except that he did it to make me over into what he wanted me to be, not to surprise me and make me happy. He coldly stated that I needed to look like "woman who is wife" for him. An hour later he threw my Bible at a window hissing, "Stop reading this crap. It's fairytale. There is no God. I am God. You must listen to me now." He was sending my Bible home as well. I would later retrieve it from the suitcase and hide it in my handbag.

As I stood in the living room hysterically admitting that I had made a huge mistake and I was terrified of him, he entered silently behind me with the two Italian brothers. I noticed that everyone was now looking past me so I turned to find him standing behind me. He stepped forward, calmly, calculatedly, and said to my mother, "Linda, she is...crazy. I try to put up with it and change her but you see that she is lying all the time. She needs help. I try to take her off your hands but...she is liar." He blew his nose awaiting agreement from my mom. At this moment my mother stepped up in the way only my mother could, and does, for all her kids.
"Miloj, my daughter may be a lot of things but one thing she's not, is a liar! We will all be leaving tomorrow." I was exuberant at my mother's defense of me. For all the confusion I had lived in the past six months I was relieved to know that she never forgot who I was. This bit of support and strength was what I had been longing for since my world crashed when River and I broke up.

He was stunned. I could tell he expected something different from my mother whom he had charmed beyond belief. Not knowing what to do next, the two brothers stepped forward telling us all how much

Miloj loved me and how we were young and needed time together on the honeymoon. Miloj, picking up on their line of reasoning, agreed and chimed in sounding filled with remorse.

"Baby I love you. I just want best for you and maybe I am stressed about my work. Please don't go. We have honeymoon trip to consider. We are husband and wife." He came over and hugged me tenderly. Just like that, with a glimmer of hope that I could turn this entire train wreck around and into the fairytale it was supposed to be, I was in again.

With that I was instructed to dress for Lenny's concert that night. He was opening for Guns N Roses at Bercy Stadium. I wanted to stay home but of course I couldn't because Miloj had invited 15 people knowing I could walk anybody I wanted in and backstage. My mom and aunt were fried and opted out of yet another late night since they were flying home the next day.

As soon as we were out of my mothers view he became cold, cruel, and distant again. His mood swings were insane. One moment he was calm and I could deal with him. The next moment he was violent and abusive verbally and physically. The mental abuse was worse than any physical abuse I had ever experienced. Worse than my childhood sexual abuse, and worse than being raped as a 15 year old girl, was Miloj's insane, cruel, mental, and verbal abuse.

By the time the night of Lenny's concert ended and we had been married for a week I was defeated, drained, demeaned, and completely lost in a marriage that was a joke. The destruction of my mind and my spirit at his hands is something I have never experienced in my entire life before or since. Lenny watched the whole thing closely all week long, continually asking me to leave when he left after his show. Now on his tour bus, the show over, he begged me to leave with him as I cried in his arms from the sheer stress of yet another night with Miloj.

"Girl, please just leave with me. Take some time. Get your head together. This cat is insane. He ain't right. Something is way off. You don't need to be left alone with him. At all."

As I walked through the airport accompanying my mom and aunt the next afternoon I was silent.
"Cynthia are you sure you don't want to leave?" I was not sure at all. In fact I knew for certain I should be leaving with them but I couldn't face defeat.
"No, mom. It's ok. I'm fine. I will be OK. Maybe we just need some time alone."

They checked in and we walked as far as I could go with them. I didn't want to stay. I was petrified to stay. But, in my very turbulent first year out of law school, I didn't want to fail again the way I felt I had failed with River. I knew I should be leaving with them. I knew I wasn't safe. I felt an overwhelming fear for my life. But, I felt caged and trapped in my own horrible reality. I hated Miloj, yet I had convinced myself I could love him if he would just go back to being the guy who relentlessly pursued me in the grocery store three months prior. I would see that guy for ten minutes a day and I would cling to that like oxygen enabling myself to stay, to keep trying, to keep hoping. I became the classic abused woman; the woman that disgusted me in movies that everyone yelled at saying leave stupid, run, get away. I was now her; a woman I completely disrespected.

I watched my mom and aunt leave, before turning around with tears running once again down my face. I was terrified and lost as I walked through the airport back to Miloj who was waiting in the car in front of Charles de Gaulle.

I got into the car quietly and stared away from him and out the window so he wouldn't see me crying. It was a long, horribly difficult, ride back. He knew I was crying yet he said nothing. He ignored me completely as he blew his nose and sniffled his way back into town. I have never felt more alone in my life. Never. Not before or since.

Suddenly he pulled up to a supermarket and stopped. He reached into his wallet and pulled something out. "Take this. Go inside and buy groceries like good wife." He shoved a credit card at me.

I mindlessly took it and went inside roaming aimlessly around the market lost in my thoughts. I selected some yoghurt, which was all I was allowed to eat without him barraging me with insults about being fat. I chose cheese and bread and a few other things, for him. I stood at the cash register waiting for the cashier to finish ringing me up. I wondered, rather annoyed, why he sent me on errands like I was his servant. When I looked up, the cashier looked at me oddly and made a call to someone.

Within minutes, a manager type walked to the register from the back somewhere. They spoke seriously in French before the gentlemen holding onto Miloj's credit card said, "May I see your passport?"
"Excuse me?"
"Your identification Madame." I gave him my passport and he looked at it and handed it back. "I must ask you to please come wait with me."
"What? Why?" I began to freak out. Something was wrong. "What's the problem?"
"This is stolen credit card Madame. And it is not you. We should wait for the police" He held the card out for me to see with an accusing look on his face. I looked at the card for the first time and realized it had a random mans name on it. I looked helplessly at the man standing before me. "I...I.. It's my husband's. I had no idea..."
"Is he with you?" I stared at him in disbelief as it dawned on me that Miloj had, knowingly, sent me into a market with a stolen credit card.

All of a sudden I bolted from the store and ran to the car. I hopped in and screamed at him hysterically. "YOU GAVE ME A STOLEN CARD." I was sobbing. Miloj started the car and we drove away.

"Where is my card?"

"It's not YOURS! Whose name was on that card? It's stolen! Why would you tell me to use a stolen credit card?"

"You lose the card. You stupid, fat, bitch...I kill you. You can't do anything right." Later that night I went inside his wallet searching for more cards or clues as to why he had me in the market with a card that had someone else's name on it. I found a handful of credit cards all of them with different names on them.

Why on earth did he marry me? Good question. I have asked that question a thousand times. I asked him a thousand times as well. A passport. A mule. An idiot he could use to gain access to my world of celebrity and celebrity friends. I didn't know. The theories would reveal themselves for years to come but I will never really know his reasons.

Why on earth did I marry him? This was an even better question. The answers became clearer and clearer as I would journey inside the world of confusion in my mind and life. I knew I was doing something stupid but I figured I could make things work out, and that all would end well no matter what. And, it was a good story that I was the star of. I craved drama at that point in my life as much as I had craved cocaine to numb my wounds the last few months. And...I wasn't thinking about River anymore with the same hurt and sadness that had dominated the prior six months. There were many reasons I married him. He was an escape route from pain I couldn't quite understand or stop. I hoped he would be the answer. In all honesty, he would be, because God knew what I did not. The biggest question of all was yet to be answered. Why on earth did God allow me to do this? If He is God and He can intervene, and does, why on earth does He show up when He finally does and in the ways He finally does? He knew my end at my beginning. And, till today, I marvel at why He felt I was so valuable.

The remaining days after everyone left went by in a blur. Miloj was focused on some business he was doing with some of the guys who were around him. They met together and spoke in many languages. I was always sent out of the room, which was fine with me. I was just trying to get through the days and minimize the arguing and the constant abuse I was experiencing. I was thoroughly afraid of him by this point and now that we were alone all I wanted to do was leave Paris and all the strange people he hung around and go on a honeymoon. Then I could fly back to the US and figure out what to do about this marriage on my own turf.

"I don't feel to live like a dog in America. You will stop dreaming of TV and get job. Real job. You have more possibilities than me. You are American attorney. I need money." He laid that on me one night. "That's not really the way God designed marriage and being a husband." I retorted.

He pushed me off of him and said defiantly, "God? Ha! How many times I tell you?! I am your God now. You will listen to me!" With that he spit into the air and laughed.

He filled me in on his plans. He liked tennis. He planned to play tennis all day while I worked. Whatever his plans were for *our* future I'm grateful God had completely different plans for *mine*.

17

LUNA DI MIELE

No temptation has overtaken you except what is common to mankind. And God is faithful; he will not let you be tempted beyond what you can bear. But when you are tempted, he will also provide a way out so that you can endure it.
1 CORINTHIANS 10:13 (NIV)

Our honeymoon began amidst hysteria and tears as Miloj raced through the South of France in a rage.
"Miloj, what is wrong? Slow down!"
"Shut up. I am sick of your questions. Stop asking me questions?" He raised his hand to hit me and I cowered in my seat.
"I thought we were going to stay in the South for our honeymoon?" I whispered suffocating on my own tears.

"I told you no more questions." I had pushed him past his limit. In that moment he swerved the car over to the side of the road and reached across me and opened my door. He began trying to push me out of the car on the side of a cliff. In the dark of the night I screamed and clung to the car as best I could promising him I would not ask any more questions. He promised that he was going to kill me when this trip was all done. I believed him. To punctuate his point, he grabbed the tiny little black kitten I had brought to Paris for him as a wedding gift, and slung it at the back window of the car. It's limp body fell in a heap to the floor. I suffocated on my tears; to terrified to do anything, or say anything, that might bring on another fit of his rage.

I sat there staring into the night thinking of God and Satan. I had dreamed about Satan the night before. It was such a disturbing dream that I woke up paralyzed with the same fear I felt now. In my dream, I was in a room and Satan had his back to me hiding his face from me. He was dressed in all black; wearing a black hat and black cape. I tapped him on the back so he would turn around. When he did, he swung the cloak from in front of his face, and it was Miloj. I gasped in my dream and actually woke myself up. I spent the rest of the night laying in bed praying. I was paralyzed by fear of what I felt the dream was saying. Now, as I accepted the fate of wherever this trip was taking me, I could only ask myself the question; did I run into the ultimate trap ever used against me in the spiritual warfare that had plagued my life since I was born?

Never before, and never since, has Satan manifested in a dream to me.

As the tears streamed silently down my face, I did the one thing I knew to do. I picked up my Bible and I read it. It was my constant companion, although I never really read it. I opened it to a scripture, which spoke of how in our times of trouble and tempting God had already prepared a way out for us. I didn't know what that 'way out' was. It never occurred to me that it was Jesus; that He had been wooing me my whole life. I knew in some way He had protected me and given me the drive to keep going forward in my life. It just never occurred to me that I had been marked by God for His purposes and that He was faithful even if I was lost, rebellious, and ignorant of what His purposes were, much less who He even was.

Suddenly, as I read, almost as if it was the reward for turning to Him, I felt a supernatural spirit of calm come over me. In that moment I knew that no matter where we were, no matter what would happen, God would never leave me. Even though I had left Him.

18

GODS RELENTLESS PURSUIT OF US

For the mountains may move and the hills disappear, but even then my faithful love for you will remain. My covenant of blessing will never be broken," says the LORD, who has mercy on you.
Isaiah 54:10 (NLT)

It often amazes me how far God went to protect me while I didn't really know Him and then to pursue me so that I would. It continues to amaze me how far He still goes to reengage my heart when it's distant and to have my time and attention, so He can bless me.

This is His promise to us. This is what undying love looks like. He relentlessly pursues us even when we are running, and hiding, and ducking, and dodging, His love. He pursues us when we are angry with Him. He pursues us when we forget Him. He pursues us when we don't even know Him. He pursues us when we are pursuing everything but Him. His love is so faithful that it is barely conceivable to us in our feeble understandings of love that anyone could so unconditionally love us and relentlessly pursue us to love us.

If I ascend up into heaven, thou art there: if I make my bed in hell, behold, thou art there
Psalm 139:8 (KJV)

Thankfully, His love is not like human love. A human would never meet you in hell on a bed you yourself made, whether knowingly or unknowingly. Humans only pursue to the point we get pursued back. God does not possess our humanness nor is he limited by our humanness. He is God and there is none like Him. I have never gotten away from His presence in my life. The free choice He gives us is in the hopes that we choose Him, but clearly the covenant He makes with us survives even our halfhearted commitment after we choose. Most would call this grace. If you don't yet know His grace I am certain you have felt His pursuit.

If you've ever experienced His presence in the form of a stranger who shares something about God with you for no apparent reason, you have experienced the grace of His pursuit. If you've ever felt the feeling that there is something more in life than what you have, you've experienced the grace of His pursuit. When you've ever had a feeling that somebody created all of what you feel couldn't exist without a God, you've experienced the grace of His pursuit. If you've ever had a realization that something has always sustained you, and even saved you, when bad things happened, then you have felt the grace of God's sweet pursuit.

He will move mountains to pursue you. He will descend into the darkest regions of whatever hell you're living in to save you. He will climb the stairs of success to rescue you from the emptiness of wealth and fame. Because His love never fails, in His grace He desires to pursue us, until we relent to His undying love for us.

But God demonstrates his own love for us in this: While we were still sinners, Christ died for us
Romans 5:8 (NIV)

An explanation of God's love for me is what my husband has given me. It was his first lesson for me on the plane when we met a decade ago and it is a lesson he has role modeled for me as a husband time after time. When someone loves you they pursue you. They don't judge your sin and shortcomings. They don't find you ugly because your lifestyle doesn't look like theirs. They don't throw you away when they deem you to have failed or been mistaken. They continue to pursue you with love and mercy. Love never fails, even when we do. And, we often do. Lets discuss love.

19

LOVE

If I speak in the tongues of men or of angels, but do not have love, I am only a resounding gong or a clanging cymbal. If I have the gift of prophecy and can fathom all mysteries and all knowledge, and if I have a faith that can move mountains, but do not have love, I am nothing. If I give all I possess to the poor and give over my body to hardship that I may boast, but do not have love, I gain nothing.
Love is patient, love is kind. It does not envy, it does not boast, it is not proud. It does not dishonor others, it is not self-seeking, it is not easily angered, it keeps no record of wrongs. Love does not delight in evil but rejoices with the truth. It always protects, always trusts, always hopes, always perseveres. Love never fails.
1 Corinthians 13 (NIV)

Wow. How's that for the definition of love that is given to us! As Christians, 1 Corinthian 13 is the loudest, boldest, action statement in the Bible. It describes love in action. It defines the love that goes to war against the plans of the enemy in our lives. The love described above is *the* battle cry that should change environments everywhere we go! When we love, according to the playbook we are provided, the world sees what it should see from us; a very peculiar people who walk in a very peculiar demonstration of love. Love that can defeat anything.

As powerful and impactful as we say we know love is, as Christians, sadly, we don't seem to walk in it, as we should. In fact, the opposite is true. When I look around the world today I see Christians walking in judgment, anger, brokenness, fear, confusion, and powerlessness, more than I see us walking in a powerful demonstration of love. I remember the old song we used to sing in Catholic school that said, "they will know we are Christians by our love, by our love. Yes, they'll know we are Christians by our love." I can hear the song as vividly as when I was a child. It marked me. I really believe, that song, coupled with my sensitivity to anyone whose been broken by other people's sin and confusion, made me able to love people in a way that is bigger than I am. Where we only see sin, love looks a bit deeper and sees pain, disillusionment, brokenness and confusion. Where we only condemn; love seeks understanding. God is love. And, God's point of view is truly all that matters. His point of view is tempered by the love described above.

I grew up wanting to be known for my love. This has given me the ability to desire to hear people's stories fully comprehending, from an early age, that everyone has a story. Everyone has something that has damaged him or her in ways invisible to the human eye, but as clear as day to Gods eye. I want to see like Him, hear like Him, feel like Him, and love like Him.

Sadly, the last thing the world knows us Christians for today is our love. At least I can speak for the U.S. which leads the world in religious freedom and sheer ability to be and do what we want on every level, including faith. We argue amongst ourselves in the U.S. over everything; whose church is correct, whose God is right, whose lifestyle choices are godly or destined for hell. Yet, few in the battle lead the way in love. There is a growing number of Christian leaders, whom I admire greatly, who understand the power of showing love to each other through unity in the church as a first necessary step in the love of Christ revealing itself.

Non-believers say Christians are judgmental, intolerant, and hateful, while they themselves, in dealing with us, act judgmental, intolerant, and hateful. Where is the group of non-believers, atheists, and alternative lifestyle supporters, that will step up and choose the superior behavior that actually expresses the non-judgment, tolerance, and love that they want, that Christians supposedly don't show them? When do two wrongs EVER make a right? The lesbians, gays, and transgenders are wrong. The atheists are wrong. The Christian's are wrong. Everybody is wrong, wrong, wrong. Everybody is living on the bottom rung of spiritual immaturity, and if I were looking from the outside in at all of us, I wouldn't choose to embrace ANY of our faiths, beliefs, or lifestyles. None of them seem powerful or appealing at all! Because, they all lack love. There is no greater definition of love than this found in God's word, and it is the love that is ours through Christ Jesus.

We are a country, and a society, that brags about our supposedly 'open minds' to embracing everyone's diverse belief's and lifestyles. Yet, let me share with you a wonderful warning a lovely Hassidic woman friend of mine shared with me, that her Rabbi shared with her; Be open, yes, but don't be so open your brains fall out your head!

In our country, and in our world today, we have embraced so much openness that our brains have literally fallen out of our heads! We find reason for what is unreasonable. Our 'Church on Sunday' hearts have gone cold for each other, and for others. We lack unity in the body because we are to focused on our differences, rather than our great common denominator; helping the world know Jesus as its Savior. As Christians we *should* know better because we *say* we embrace the Word of God that preaches love, non-judgment, and unity. We must never be so open we embrace the stupidity that clouds our chief goal; to make disciples of Christ and to share His love.

As the body of Christ we need to wake up and actually do our jobs; be servants of a Most Holy High God, preach the gospel of Jesus in love, and pray for others, heal the sick, feed the poor, and raise the dead. Instead of imparting life, and love, everywhere we go, we for the most part, because of complete spiritual immaturity and ignorance of our own playbook, allow ourselves to be used to sew dissension, hatred, division, and confusion. I have never seen more Christian leaders that look like the world in my life. I left the world to be a weapon of love and power in the kingdom and it looks virtually the same over here as it does over there guys. Problem. Don't we, as the church body, see that it is wrong that the last thing we are known by is our love?

Can I prove this? Yes!

My assertion is simple to prove because when you look around you'll see that the majority of Christian's today don't really relentlessly pursue anyone, not even God. For a gospel that men have died for, traveled the earth to share, and suffered torture because of, we have become less bold about lovingly and dedicatedly sharing our faith in all situations, less clearly identifiable as Christians, less anointed with Gods power, and less infatuated with Jesus.

As we have fallen out of love with our faith, we have fallen out of love with Jesus. As we have fallen out of love with Jesus, we have fallen out of love with people. As we have fallen out of love with people we have less interest in loving, or pursuing, them. Passionate love directly impacts the strength and vigor of our pursuit of anything; especially others.

"Neither height nor depth, nor anything else in all creation, will be able to separate us from the love of God that is in Christ Jesus our Lord. "
Romans 8:39 (NIV)

What a promise. His love, unlike ours, never fails. Even when we fail each other and even where we are failing the world, right now today. His love never fails. Because of that, and only that, we have the hope of victory and the joy of overcoming our own weaknesses. Jesus Christ is the same yesterday, today, and forever. Because of Him, and His unchanging love, there is hope that we as a body can unite and demonstrate the life changing, community changing, power of His love. Jesus spent his last moments on earth praying for us to be unified, to effectively be, the light of the world as He was. In His last moments He thought only of us. It was all about us for Him. It is still all about us to Him. This is the patient, merciful, kind, love that is ours to receive and ours to powerfully give to others.

This is cause for great joy if you've been wounded by humans, hurt by the church, disillusioned with authority. His covenant of blessing will never be broken, by any person, circumstances, or events that try and wage war against Him. We are loved with His undying love that possesses His undying power. It's time for us to be known by our love, because more than ever, others need to know His love. If we refuse to be a vessel of His love then who will be?

I can answer that question easily also. I will tell you who will gladly be a vessel supplying the void that is left inside when His love is nowhere to be found to fill it; Satan. The mere statement sounds kooky. Satan?! But, yes, I say it again. We have a very real enemy after us throughout our lives. His goal is deceit, confusion, and destruction. He will fill your void with a lust for fame, people, sex, drugs, anything to make you feel loved, all the while poisoning your system and projecting his identity onto you while stealing yours.

What will you do right now to change?

What will you do right now today to ensure that each day you are seeking spiritual knowledge of the Word and will of God so that your spiritual immaturity will not keep you from being a source of love in the world?

What will you do today to stop turning off others to any desire to know the loving, awesome, amazing, God who loves, not just YOU, but all those you find impossible to love?

What will you do to stop seeking your own shine and let Gods light shine brighter?

Will you choose to love others the way God loves you as defined in 1 Corinthians 13?

If you do, the world will change!

The one thing I know for certain that God has placed on my heart the last year is the message found in 2 Chronicles 7:14. It is a message for us believers, not for everybody else we've focused on.

This message, I strongly believe, is the number one answer to the world's pain, hatred, confusion, and chaos. This message is the way we as believers will ignite the love in us, and around us, that the world needs to see and know us by. The message is simple and *we* are the answer!

"Then if MY people who are called by my name will humble themselves and pray and seek my face and turn from their wicked ways, I will hear from heaven and will forgive their sins and restore their land."
2 Chronicles 7:14 (NLT)

We are the ones responsible for the spiritual climate in the world today. *We* are the ones to blame for the spiritual malaise and lack of interest in being Christian. *We* are the reason for the virtual non-existence of power, signs and wonders, flowing like rushing rivers through every room we walk in. *We* are the ones guilty of the simple fact that as Christians today, they do not know us by our love.
It is time for us to repent. It is time for us to turn from the selfish ways in which we've dropped the ball. It is time for unity in the body and a coming together of the power amongst us based on our shared fundamental beliefs more than our differences. It is time to let the

world see the changes that occur when Love walks in the room and into each person's life we, as the unified Body of Christ, encounter!

The world is waiting. He is waiting. For love to show up.

Why do you suppose He is waiting for us to understand this?

This one is simple again. He wants us to understand where we are today and to know what's coming tomorrow. I believe strongly that He is issuing a warning with instructions to us to release His last great stand in revival.

When I shut up the heavens so that there is no rain, or command locusts to devour the land or send a plague among my people, if my people, who are called by my name, will humble themselves and pray and seek my face and turn from their wicked ways, then I will hear from heaven, and I will forgive their sin and will heal their land. Now my eyes will be open and my ears attentive to the prayers offered in this place. I have chosen and consecrated this temple so that my Name may be there forever. My eyes and my heart will always be there.
2 Chronicles 7:13-22 (NIV)

We are His temple aren't we?! His name rests with us, and in us, as Christians. His eyes and His heart are always with us and on us. His eyes and heart are also available to others because of us.

Do you complain that the laws of the land do not uphold Gods laws? Do you worry about the fate of Christians and who will actually lead with our principles? I think we need to spend less time worrying, and more time praying, and living the way *we* are supposed to. We are His temple. We are the environment changers. Let's get busy changing the environment by changing ourselves.

The gifts and supernatural powers His love provides us, while amazing, mean very little because they will all pass away leaving only three things.

And now these three remain: faith, hope and love. But the greatest of these is love.
1 Corinthians 13:13 (NIV)

Love. Need I say more?! We have turned our backs on love. Love has turned His back on us! If we humble ourselves and repent love will save us. Love will heal our lands and restore us to the position of power we are intended to be in. Love.

The greatest thing is love. It is all up to us!

20

THE DRIVE HOME

Leaving the crowd, they took Him along with them in the boat, just as He was; and other boats were with Him. And there arose a fierce gale of wind, and the waves were breaking over the boat so much that the boat was already filling up. Jesus Himself was in the stern, asleep on the cushion; and they woke Him and said to Him, "Teacher, do You not care that we are perishing?" And He got up and rebuked the wind and said to the sea, "Hush, be still." And the wind died down and it became perfectly calm. And He said to them, "Why are you afraid? Do you still have no faith?" They became very much afraid and said to one another, "Who then is this, that even the wind and the sea obey Him?"
Mark 4:36-41 (NASB)

I slept as we drove silently through the night, only halfway waking up when I felt Miloj nudge my legs for me to move them. I drew them up to my chest and curled up in a ball in my seat so he could rummage around under my feet. I avoided eye contact by turning and closing my eyes to go back to sleep. I was determined to play so small I disappeared from his view. I finally realized he did not love me, I did not love myself, and this entire choice was about anything but love.

By the time we drove into a little port town called Cagliari, Miloj's stress levels were at an all time high. He was yelling at me. Pushing me. Calling me names. Threatening me. He acted more erratic than he had in the entire ten days of hell I had been in with him. He barely slept, barely ate, and blew his nose continuously all day and night. Retreating to use the bathroom constantly, he sniffed at me that he had kidney problems that were bothering him, when I questioned his constant disappearing. He was a mess. I was exhausted and scared so I tried to stay calm and stay quiet. My questions only sent him into orbit and by this point I was completely convinced that he intended to make good on his promise to kill me when this was all over. Whatever 'this' was, I was now plotting how to get away.

My plan was to call Lenny and make my way to his tour bus somewhere in Europe and leave this maniac I had married behind. Then I would curl up next to my 'brother' until I healed mentally, spiritually, and emotionally.

21

SISTER

As iron sharpens iron, so a friend sharpens a friend
Proverbs 27:17 (NLT)

There is such ultimate truth in this scripture. The friendships in our lives need to constantly push us to go higher and deeper in our relationships with Christ. Just as bad company corrupts good character so also does great company encourage, support, strengthen, and nurture, good character. As if we are iron, being rubbed together, a Godly friendship should and does sharpen each other.

Part of the issues I was plagued with prior to being saved, and even after, as you'll see in reading this book, had everything to do with the company I kept. Of course, those closest to me have always been good people, great people even. However, they weren't necessarily knowledgeable people about living a life surrendered in every way to Jesus as the Boss of your life. They weren't living this way and so they couldn't much teach what they themselves didn't know. There were some around who could have provided instruction if I had realized I needed to push for more, I suppose. But, because I was so focused on my career I gravitated toward my career friends, and I relied on my own limited spiritual knowledge of what was right and wrong. In all honesty, I also found Christians to be weird, not very well traveled, and therefore un-relatable to me, and the world I perceived as mine.

What I did have were a couple very close friends, who were basically baby Christians like I was, who at least encouraged me to be the best *me* I could be.

One such person is my brother and close friend, Lenny. He didn't care for Miloj at all and he was certainly concerned about my moment on the edge of confusion. He saw a lot of people around me whom I could sense he felt were hangers-on and not *ideal* company. Then again he journeyed through many people like this also in that season of life.

Lenny and I started calling each other brother and sister sometime in high school, around fifteen years old, although I don't really remember when. He got radically saved at that time and this is the reason, I'm sure, he was able to see Jesus in me, and the calling on my life. God made a covenant that included us before we would ever realize it; of this I am certain.

Having known each other since we were really young we shared, and share, so many things in common it's hard to include other people in our history. My husband is the only man I have ever known, or been with, whose not on some level intimidated by Lenny's pure presence, much less his talent and his obvious role in my heart and life. I think labeling each other brother and sister was our way of protecting whatever we had, and wanting the world to leave us alone, and not try and limit what we share with its very limited labels when trying to comprehend deep relationships between men and women.

We have never lived in a box, or a category, neither personally as individuals, and certainly not as two people who love each other deeply. I believe that God sanctified our relationship from day one allowing us to never cross lines that could destroy the destiny He had in our lives concerning each other. He has seen me at my best. He has seen me at my worst. More than anyone in my life he has 'seen' me. As I have him.

Because he has always seen the real 'me', and because, at many times, certainly the time I ran off in a world of confusion and married a virtual stranger, he has seen more in me than I often did in myself, I have lived with the greatest validation and encouragement of who I am as a girl, a mother, and a woman of God. Truth be told, I have always felt so powerful because of him, because he never cared or needed me to be doing anything with my life except be the best me that I could be.

'Me,' was always smart enough, talented enough, funny enough, and beautiful enough. With my ailing self-esteem for many years, this was incredibly healing to me. In my world, which was filled with that rather *Hollywood* need to explain what project, or people, validated your worth, I have always felt priceless and valuable to *him*. He has been closer than a brother, as steadfast in supporting me as a husband, shared more intimacy with me than any ex-lover, and ridden more highs and lows with me than any other friend. The safety net of peace and calm Lenny provided in my life then, and now, is something I'm sure we both know can't ever be replaced because God has truly used our relationship.

Having people like this in your life is important. I would encourage you to look closely at the people you surround yourself with, not just at school or work, but also in your personal time. These are the people that will contribute to your rising or falling in life. They will assist you when you fall. They will pull you gently back down to earth when your feet have completely left the ground.

Write down their names on a list. Write a brief description of the common bonds you share. Do they challenge you to be a better Christian? Do they have the knowledge to help you be one? If your bonds are about anything other than Jesus, at the very core, you should check *your* motives for being in their lives, and you should check *their* motives for being in yours. Your motives should be about witnessing Gods love to them and being ready always to help them know the love of Jesus Christ that is theirs to salvation. Friendship should be based in fruit, the ultimate goal of fruit, or the watering of seeds that have already been planted, in the hopes of one day bearing fruit. Love should be pre-eminent. Friendship based in anything less than this has left God out of the equation. And only God matters; for without God there is no equation on earth that will ultimately matter. You can build skyscrapers together. You can amass earthly wealth and fleshly pleasure but a friendship not rooted in Gods will is ultimately never satisfying.

As I have grown to love myself and see the greatness in me, that Lenny has always seen, our relationship has grown to new heights. I am grateful that I made it to the place my mom Roxie, his mother, told me to make it to before she died. She told me to, "Love him but never be afraid to risk losing him in order to be his real friend and sister." She understood by the time she passed away, that he had become very famous. As his fame increased she knew there would be fewer and fewer people in his life that would risk losing the perks of being his friend to actually *be* his friend. I didn't understand that as a younger girl, but as a woman I have learned, through the years, what that statement really meant.

Love may be never having to say your sorry, but it sure isn't never saying things that you may be made to feel sorry about saying. A friend, especially one who is a brother or sister in Christ, cannot hold back the hard stuff. You have to keep it real with each other, even when the truth hurts, because hardly anyone else will have the ability to navigate the conversation. A union, in which iron is truly sharpening iron, walks the unique road of delivering the truth in love, while encouraging each other to walk correctly in the truth of wherever you are on a given day.

My prayer and my commitment to him is the one I made to my 'mom Roxie' whom I got to disciple for years before she passed; that we will always push each other higher, grow each other to be stronger, and stand by each other when everyone else has left and all the music has faded away. And, the music surely fades away.

While the life we live, has been fun, I no longer care about red carpets with him, because I am there when he returns from walking on them. I prefer to provide an honest appraisal of whether his walk is as strong as it should be and as in line with the calling God has on his life as it can be. Through our successes and failures, fame and cancer, our marriages and divorces, childbirth and child rearing, the only thing that matters to me where Leonard Albert Kravitz is concerned is his happiness and true growth in Jesus Christ by whom he too has been saved.

Even now, he is in the studio working, and I am sitting in his house, down the street from mine, on the beach writing this book. We are both living through unique transitions, and as I find safety and familiarity with him through mine, God seems to be using me to provide help and support through his. That's what friends are for. Through it all, we have a constant barrage of questions to reflect upon, and find answers for, as we seek Gods will in all of it. We continue to try and be as iron to each other, sharpening our swords of warfare, to battle through to the victory of each of our individual callings in Christ Jesus.

I encourage you, as you think about friendship, and brothers and sisters in Christ, to reflect upon the blessing they are from God, to aid us in knowing Him better, and walking more strongly. This recognition of God in your relationships will cause you to walk in destiny with a clearer purpose and vision. Through the experiences discussed in this book, I have truly learned of the importance of the people God has placed near me and allowed to remain near me.

Do not be misled: "Bad company corrupts good character."
1 Corinthians 15:33 (NLT)

God can truly use relationships with others to help shape and define you for His ultimate purposes, just as Satan can use relationships to help distract, destroy, and delay you from His ultimate purposes.

As Lenny's mom, my mom Roxie, used to always say; people are in your life for a season, a reason, or a lifetime. I'm confident enough through the testing of time that Lenny and I are 'lifers.'

Since he expresses himself tremendously through his music nothing has touched me more than the day I was sitting in my room at the residence, pregnant, and in need of communication from home. My my phone rang.
"Hey girl." I knew right away who it was and I could tell immediately he was excited about something.
"Hey babe. Whatcha doin?" Ninety nine times out of a hundred his voice makes me smile.
"I just finished in the studio. I wrote you something. I wanna sing it to you. It's amazing."
"You wrote something for me?"
" Yep. Listen." With only his guitar and his voice he sang a beautiful and haunting song he had written for me, called 'Sister.' I cried.

SISTER
Lenny Kravitz

Sister
Did you have to fall in love
With a man
That never was

Up to no good
He took your soul
And he stole your only heart
Flipped your wig and left a permanent scar

Sister
Did you have to go away
You left your home
And the things you had to say

It didn't feel good to let you slide
I never got to say goodbye
I miss you girl I think I'm gonna cry

If they knock on your door
You already gave
You don't need no more of what's ailing you
Just lean on your soul with all that it takes

May god bring you back home to America
America, America, America, America.

Sister, sister, sister, sister, sister
It's just a test of faith
Your heart is pure so the devil's in your face
I'll see you soon
'Cause they haven't got a case
And you'll be free
In a beautiful place, in a beautiful place
In a beautiful place, in a beautiful place

If they knock on your door
You already gave

22

HELP I NEED SOMEBODY

Then they cried to the LORD in their trouble, And He brought them out of their distresses. He caused the storm to be still, So that the waves of the sea were hushed. Then they were glad because they were quiet, So He guided them to their desired haven.
Psalm 107:28-30 (NASB)

The door burst open as I was trying frantically to communicate with the front desk staff from the phone in our room. I wanted to call home. He grabbed the phone hanging it up.

"WHERE IS IT?" Miloj hissed at me returning from meeting God only knows whom.

"I don't know." I sobbed. "I threw it out."

"You do what?"

"I took the car while you were gone and I drove up the side of the hill and I threw it away, Miloj!!! I don't want anything to do with this. Why did you bring me with you? This is supposed to be our honeymoon!"

"You idiot?" He raised his hand menacingly. "We are in military zone. They have eyes everywhere. People watching." He dragged me to the balcony and waved his hand outside as if to show me. "You have no idea what I am doing. You don't know these people. I need my stuff. They will kill you. I will kill you when this is finished. I will *kill* You! You will find it. NOW!" He snatched me by the arm, twisting it with such force I yelped in pain. "Lets go! NOW!!!" He was reeling. As I watched him literally melt down it was clear he had reached the end of a rope he intended to hang me with.

What I never told him, as he pulled me crying and pleading onto the balcony, was that I saw what looked like police in the same spot I had thrown his packages. They had found them. I wanted to be found and helped by someone much more than I cared what it would take to prove my innocence over the course of the following years. I wanted to be free of him, and my life with him. I wanted to be free, especially, of the black leather packages that were filled with cocaine; a kilo of it.

The irony of him being a drug dealer hit me like a ton of bricks as he spit curses at me while pulling me down the road, on the side of the cliff, near our hotel. I had left my spiraling life in search of a Savior from the glamorous world of celebrity friends and cocaine I had fallen into because River and I broke up...for this?! It just couldn't be true I remember thinking. All I could think about was the lie I told him, just a few months earlier, on the morning after we slept together, about ever using cocaine so that he would respect me and not judge the out of control moment I was in because I had a broken heart and a temporarily broken life. I flew across the world and married him because the two months after he left me alone in LA sent me on a downward spiral into cocaine and alcohol abuse that got so bad I was afraid it would kill me. He was supposed to be my Savior from the madness brought on by my broken heart. He was supposed to fix my life, at least for the moment. Truth be told, he was supposed to provide a whole new identity because mine had seemed non-existent for months. This entire relationship with him was supposed to be drama, yes. But, it was supposed to be good drama.

I tried to look normal while fear and panic gripped my heart. My face was stained with tears as he pulled me past the front desk and outside the hotel doors. He was squeezing my arm so hard I thought it would snap. The pain of his grip was searing through my body.
"Act normal or I kill you now."
He pulled me onto the road walking in the direction I had pointed to the drugs. He cursed and spit and hissed at me, for what seemed like an eternity, until we had walked a half-mile or so up the side of a hill that plunged down into the ocean.

"Where is it?" He screamed at me.

"I don't know." I cried. "Miloj, please you're hurting me. Let me go."

"Shutup." He scanned the road up and down the hillside frantically searching for his black leather packages. After walking in circles forever, the hotel was far in the distance as dusk was approaching. "There!" I yelled hoping he would let go of my arm at least long enough to retrieve his stuff. Visible in a ditch in the middle of a hillside of weeds and bushes and sand I could see black leather. Afraid I would run away, He pulled me down into the ditch with him and grabbed his bag with the packages in it. He then pulled me out of the ravine with him. With his bag in one hand and my arm in his other he dragged me back toward the hotel.

"Don't you see? There are eyes everywhere. We are in military zone you dumb, stupid..." Before he could finish, racing toward us in the distance, was a caravan of black SUV's. They had red lights flashing and sirens blaring. The Carabinieri. The Italian military police.

For all the insanity of that fateful day I have come to realize that the details don't matter. They never mattered even while I was living them. What mattered most was 'why' I was living them in the first place. What was I really running from? And why was I running so hard, and so fast, that I ran right into this man, who exploited my stupidity, and the fact that I was running to fast and to blind to see where I was going.

Even now I have my theories about why he was doing what he was doing, why he married me, and why he thought I would be down for him selling cocaine. But, that doesn't matter either. My father raised me to never be a victim, and my mother showed me by example how not to be one, so all that really mattered now was why on earth I took my life so for granted that I ran off with a man I didn't know, married him, and ended up in jail with him. I was tired running. I was out of false gods to focus on to numb my pain and soothe my wounds. I had avoided my own issues long enough. I desperately needed to know

God and His point of view on everything that had happened and was currently happening in my life; if there was a God. Why was I here? Why did I hurt so deeply? How did I allow this to happen? What was I supposed to learn? I would have very little energy left to focus on Miloj. I would soon have, and need, all my energy to focus on myself.

Sitting in the back of a black SUV, one of many in the caravan now racing through the streets of Cagliari, sirens blaring, heart pounding, and head spinning, all Miloj could say to me was, "It's finished. I'm over. I hate you! You ruin my life."

I ruined *his* life? We were surrounded by God knows how many armed military police, called Carabinieri, while he was holding a bag, that we finally found and retrieved from down in the ditch where I had thrown it, with *his* kilo of cocaine spilling out of it. But, *I* ruined *his* life. The irony of that statement almost made me laugh out loud. Guess who was playing the victim?!

After two days of being interrogated in a holding cell by men who spoke no English I was emotionally on the verge of mental collapse. Miloj spoke for himself, and for me, initially, so I wouldn't have any idea until a month later, while sitting in prison, that he had tried to put the blame on me and my rock and roll brother. My attorney later told me that he actually tried to say the drugs were mine. Thankfully the police found this one to be as hilarious as I did, and still do.

What is even more hilarious is the way he cycled in and out of personalities and angles to force me to help him.

"My love." He switched into whatever different person he needed to be to manipulate me. "They will separate us now. You must support me. Say nothing. My love you are my life. I need you to be good Christian girl and don't abandon me. I have no one; just you. Please say to your family and Lenny to help me too. They say they are Christians. They must respect I am your husband. We must stay together. Tell to them they must pay attorney to help us both as one. You and husband are one. God say it. Be good girl." He tried every angle in the book.

Eventually, I was called into a room alone with what must have been the Captain, and another man named Marco, who was the kindest man you could ever meet in a mess like I was in. He spoke English, which is why they called him in to speak with me, after 28 hours of me sitting there listening to a language I didn't understand and hoping Miloj was translating everything to me. I could tell immediately that Marco desperately wanted me to be able to tell him *something* or give him some information so they could send me home.

He said they were expecting Miloj, and a large traffic of drugs, to be setting up in and out of the island. They explained that he had stamps from Turkey in his passport where I surely would've been hung for drug trafficking. They said his modeling career was all a front to get in and out of other countries, and that an American passport, which he would get by marrying me, was very valuable. They said he likely planned to dump my body on the side of a road and that all I was to him was entre into a privileged world of success and celebrity that he planned to exploit. They said he was reputedly involved in an organization that was trafficking drugs around the world to buy arms for the current Serbian civil war going on. This information came from a group called the Balkan Group out of Paris that was supposedly investigating him. They said I would get twenty years if I didn't give them some information to help them. They said so many things.

I was so dumb-founded and lost in this situation that most people, myself included, blamed me for very little, except utter stupidity. A huge crime in my opinion. They all realized that in those initial hours when we were separated, and I was unable to speak for myself, I was clueless to Miloj attempting to do, what we call in the states, a virtual hatchet job on me. Further evidence of my stupidity.

Marcos last words to me were something about being like Bambi locked in the headlights, unable to move, and get out of the way. This was such an odd statement to me, because I've always wondered how, and why, when deer get locked into a cars headlights they can't move, leaving them susceptible to being hit and killed. Are they paralyzed and unable to move out of the way because of fear, or the lights, or what exactly is it that causes them to stand there staring head on at their own death?

With little information I could provide to help the police, and free myself from Miloj's nightmare, we were both delivered to Buoncammino prison. He was taken to be processed into the men's side and I was escorted to be processed into the women's side. Except for the few times I would see him at various trials and court dates, I would never see him again.

I watched him be lead away into the night. He was cold, defeated, angry, and even sad. I prayed nonstop while the tears streaming silently down my face became the only thing I could communicate about what I was feeling. I felt bad for him. I felt bad for myself. I was so conflicted about what I was supposed to feel.

They eventually escorted me from the main reception area to an infirmary where I was put through a ton of medical exams and blood tests. I managed to understand them asking questions about whether I was pregnant, to which I said no, but they made me take two forms of a pregnancy test anyway. The one in which I had to pee on a stick was negative. The other came back negative as well.

When my cell door locked late that night, two days after our arrest, I stood alone in a stone room. There was a window with bars covering it at the end of the room and a bunk bed. I climbed up top and lay there silently. I hadn't slept in days, months actually. I was beyond tired. I was spiritually exhausted in the very depth of my being. My spirit was completely broken and totally defeated. I had no hope left for any of the little girl dreams I once had. I sat there realizing that perhaps everything I thought my life would be was now over before it ever began. I stared into the small room with only the light of the moon as my light bulb. And, I cried. I cried. And, I cried. And, I cried. I suffocated my sobs, into my pillow, not wanting anyone to hear up and down the cold corridors of Buoncammino Prison; my new home.

"God," I whispered into the night. "If you're real, if you really are there, then please help me. Please talk to me. If I'm here for twenty years like they're saying then please tell me what you want from me now."

There were no more people, no more distractions, no more games to play with myself, or anyone else. There was only God and me now. I had travelled to the other side of the world, to a different country, to a different land, to find what I needed all along; silence and time alone with Him. It took all this to get me to confront my faith. Did I believe in God or did I not? My mouth would have certainly said I did. My actions evidenced that I did not.

It is from this initial question that all things would finally flow. Is God real? Did I believe enough to follow Him? Did I trust Him with my life and with all things concerning my life? And, if He existed, and if I believed in Him, who was He really?

He had finally gotten me all to Himself. He wanted to meet me as much as I needed to meet Him.

It took all this to finally get me to take the journey home to my Father's house; where I would find out not just who He was, but who I was.

23

FAITH

Now faith is the substance of things hoped for, the evidence of things not seen. For by it the elders obtained a good report. Through faith we understand that the worlds were framed by the word of God, so that things which are seen were not made of things which do appear.
Hebrews 11:1-3 (KJV)

What exactly does it mean to have faith?

Faith is the evidence of things unseen. Interesting to put it this way indeed. How could something you don't see have evidence to prove its there? How can something you can't know leave proof that it can be known? These are big questions with even bigger answers.

When you look at the Bible in its entirety and the words of the prophets, over thousands of years, you prove the existence of God and His son, Jesus Christ, as the risen from the dead Savior of the world. Please don't attempt an argument to the contrary unless and until you've, at bare minimum, done this. That would be ignorant. One cannot conclude the facts of a thing without first investigating the thing.

But proving God and proving Jesus is not at issue here in this chapter. Faith and what it is and looks like is. It is the substance of things hoped for and the evidence of things we cannot see.

I believed in God. I believed in Jesus. The issue is, I didn't look or act like I did. Because, in all honesty, I was playing the God of my own life.

I was going my own way, doing my own thing, in response to my own feelings. I was trying various ways to heal myself and understand myself instead of asking God for healing and understanding. Why? If I knew Him then why was I living in this way? Because, I didn't really *know* Him, *believe* in Him, or *trust* Him on any real level.

This mere acquaintance with God is where most people are content to live. It leaves them with no choice but to be Lord of their own lives, which is comfortable to most people anyway. Most people do not have the courage to live their lives according to faith. Faith takes great courage.

It was by faith that Moses' parents hid him for three months when he was born. They saw that God had given them an unusual child, and they were not afraid to disobey the king's command.
It was by faith that Moses, when he grew up, refused to be called the son of Pharaoh's daughter. He chose to share the oppression of God's people instead of enjoying the fleeting pleasures of sin. He thought it was better to suffer for the sake of Christ than to own the treasures of Egypt, for he was looking ahead to his great reward. It was by faith that Moses left the land of Egypt, not fearing the king's anger. He kept right on going because he kept his eyes on the one who is invisible. It was by faith that Moses commanded the people of Israel to keep the Passover and to sprinkle blood on the doorposts so that the angel of death would not kill their firstborn sons. It was by faith that the people of Israel went right through the Red Sea as though they were on dry ground. But when the Egyptians tried to follow, they were all drowned. It was by faith that the people of Israel marched around Jericho for seven days, and the walls came crashing down. It was by faith that Rahab the prostitute was not destroyed with the people in her city who refused to obey God. For she had given a friendly welcome to the spies. How much more do I need to say? It would take too long to recount the stories of the faith of Gideon, Barak, Samson, Jephthah, David, Samuel, and all the prophets. By faith these people overthrew

135

kingdoms, ruled with justice, and received what God had promised them. They shut the mouths of lions, quenched the flames of fire, and escaped death by the edge of the sword. Their weakness was turned to strength. They became strong in battle and put whole armies to flight. Women received their loved ones back again from death.
But others were tortured, refusing to turn from God in order to be set free. They placed their hope in a better life after the resurrection. Some were jeered at, and their backs were cut open with whips. Others were chained in prisons. Some died by stoning, some were sawed in half, and others were killed with the sword. Some went about wearing skins of sheep and goats, destitute and oppressed and mistreated. They were too good for this world, wandering over deserts and mountains, hiding in caves and holes in the ground.
Hebrews 11:23-38 (NLT)

These hall of famers, in the Bible, followed the voice and word of God in all things.

One must only read not just Hebrews 11, but the entire Bible, to see the great battles fought and won, the martyred lives of men who chose torture and death over renouncing the truth of God and Christ, and the kingdoms and people who moved from one place to the next receiving Gods promises to them, to know that something is at work that is bigger than all of us. Even those who didn't receive their promises in this lifetime went to their deaths assuredly knowing they would receive them after. Their absolute faith in what they knew God told them changed the world, and provided an example, for us all, of what it means to trust God absolutely.

And, while He relentlessly pursues us, He is quite the gentleman. The *choice* He leaves up to you. You can allow Him to be God and have faith that He really is who He says He is, and He really can do what He says He can do, or not.

If your answer is that you do not believe in God, then there is very little journey left really. You live, and you will die, and you alone will fill the pages of your life unaided by anyone, or anything, except those around you whose answers you will have no choice but to find trustworthy. You will, I pray, find the sufficient ability within yourself to either not ask any questions about what you don't know, or the intellect to answer every question that nobody else, and likely even yourself, honestly have no answer for. When you choose to have no faith, There is so much you are choosing to leave to chance to navigate, without any depth of wisdom, on your own. What normally happens, in my experiences, is that people eventually crumble under the weight of what they cannot do, understand, or overcome, on their own, and in their own strength.

Most people eventually come to the place in life where they realize, even in a moment they toss aside, that they themselves are lacking any real power to control their destiny's, change their pasts, or overcome their deepest struggles. At this place, God is always there pursuing, offering, hoping and waiting, for His children to take one step toward knowing Him and receiving all that He has promised.

24

ALL ARE WELCOME

Then Jesus said, "Come to me, all of you who are weary and carry heavy burdens, and I will give you rest. Take my yoke upon you. Let me teach you, because I am humble and gentle at heart, and you will find rest for your souls. For my yoke is easy to bear, and the burden I give you is light."
Matthew 11:28-30 (NLT)

In Gods battle to win my soul, and in His relentless pursuit of me, I am still amazed at how easy living for Him really is. I guess I always thought that if I didn't make my own decisions and take my own actions then things wouldn't get done in my life. I had fought since childhood to survive, deep in my spirit, which was under severe emotional attack from the distress caused by my sexual abuse and, like most people, I now realize, I had to learn to let go and let God shoulder my burdens while I actually shouldered only the ones He gave me; to know Him and to trust Him. These are extremely easy and non-burdensome requirements.

However, while I was carrying my burdens, like a huge weight around my neck, I was shackled to a past that was hurting me and anchored to brokenness that was threatening to destroy the call on my future. I was utterly exhausted from the constant war I had lived in for many years. I was incapable of winning on my own. I tried every way, and every remedy, imaginable. Nothing worked. I was wrestling ghosts and shadow boxing with demons from my past and my present and it all served to destroy my future; if not my very life.

The weight of life can easily overwhelm you. The weight of all that we live and go through is an extremely heavy weight to bear alone. Even other people never lift the load completely. Only my relationship with God has ever lifted the load completely; providing peace when there should be none and joy when sorrow looms.

It is actually all a faith issue. We carry our heavy burdens alone when we don't believe there is a God to help us. When we do believe there is God to help us, we run to Him with everything. Before a burden becomes to heavy, He lifts it, and replaces it with promises we can trust in. When we believe that God is our Father and that Jesus is our Savior we understand that the Holy Spirit lives in us and we are guided into all truth in time. God will fight our battles we learn. Then we learn to sit and watch Him win on our behalf. I am actually far more capable today, then ten years ago even, to sit in faith and wait for God to act on my behalf. You get better with time.

This doesn't exonerate you from action because faith is very much an action. But, it does cause you to wait for God to signal action or to know that God warrants action, before moving a single inch.

The sum total of all this is that you no longer carry the burden of your past but the hope of your tomorrows with Him.

25

OUR TO DO LISTS

"For the word of God is alive and active. Sharper than any double-edged sword, it penetrates even to dividing soul and spirit, joints and marrow; it judges the thoughts and attitudes of the heart."
Hebrews 4:12 (NIV)

God's words, when spoken, never cease to amaze me. Like the scripture above says, they cut right to the very core of a person issues. You cannot escape the wisdom of them. They are supernaturally empowered and never return void of Gods intended results when they are spoken to others. When you see the supernaturally empowered word of God, moving through someone's heart like a tidal wave, I don't understand how we don't spend more time knowing the Bible inside and out. God's words are life, love, and power. I can listen to many conversations with many people, even my husband, but it is only God's word that goes deep inside me revealing to me the thoughts and intentions of my very own heart better than I could myself. When His word brings revelation to the hearer, as it always does, always, it is impossible to escape Gods wisdom, which often brings shockingly deep conviction in areas. It exposes wounds, and ugliness, as much as it blesses and encourages what is good and beautiful inside us. Only God truly knows us. Only He knows what we need to hear and when we need to hear it. Therefore, His word speaks powerfully, and truthfully, to us as individuals.

This is actually one reason why people run from hearing His word or learning His word. It's why people allow distraction in every form to come against their alone time with Him. Because sometimes the truth hurts. Sometimes we don't want to hear it. Sometimes we just aren't ready to see ourselves as clearly as God does. I have met people who prefer to stay in a holding pattern called stupidity and stagnate in their immaturity and when I do I can only shake my head. Willful ignorance is insanity.

Then there are those who knowingly, and unknowingly, partner with the enemy of their lives, repeatedly, by allowing themselves to be distracted. He works hard to keep us to busy to sit and spend time with God. When our laziness, or busyness, gets in the way of our relationship with God, yet again, we say to Him in our actions that spending time alone with Him is a waste of time. It must be, when we don't do it, since it is very clear that Gods *word* will transform a life and change a heart bringing it out of darkness and confusion into light and victory.

However, like many today, I am easily distracted and constantly thinking to much about the days to-do list or the ideas I feel lead to give birth to. I have to fight the onslaught of thoughts that arrive each morning like a wave crashing on the shore of my home, in Malibu, even right now. The temptation exists to just begin the day writing, excited to finish this book that I believe God wants me to write and share with others. Even in this, I remember that I need to pull away and start my day with Him because He has bigger things, than even the list of things He has given me charge over, that He needs my attention about.

This knowledge, that He must be first in order to achieve anything successfully, is very humbling. It's a battle to break free from the pull of the distractions, to alone time with Him. But, when I do it's glorious. It's as if the peace of God personally settles over me. I often cry because the struggle in my Spirit to still my mind and get in Gods presence has been so overwhelmingly powerful. Yet, He has taught me, time after time, that what He wants is to bless me with so much more than just the answers to the questions that are whirling around inside me daily.

God knows our questions. He has the answers. All He wants is our attention so that he can truly be God, a good Father, in our lives. He wants to lead us into all kinds of victories that will not only speak the truth of Him, but also glorify Him, while providing the desires of our hearts. This, my friends, is amazing.

I understand this struggle in the Spirit, really well, to be close to God. And know this much, the enemy of your life doesn't want it to happen.

Why?

Because, as I've explained inadvertently, power lies in *relationship*!

God's power becomes your power when you are in a personal relationship with *Him*. In relationship, you know that He is not dead but very much alive, and that His word truly does heal the broken-hearted and set the captives free. Satan wants you held captive. He wants you enslaved to your brokenness and your lack of knowledge. If it were not for even the little relationship I had with God, back when my life turned upside down, I would have probably killed myself. It's that simple.

Because of this knowledge, religion alone will never be worth my time, my hope, or my future. In my experiences, I have ultimately learned that religion, absent a personal relationship with God, is worth little.

I, like many, have seen the hypocrisy in religion. I, like many, have seen that religion can fail time after time. But when you realize that God is not in religion, but that He is found in relationship, all of a sudden you realize how important it is for *you* personally to know Him. This personal relationship with your Father is so much bigger than your religion. God never fails. God never endorses religion. However, He endorses people over and over and over again. We are His church, His body, and His bride. Religion, a man-made phenomenon, will pass away. But we, His children, will live forever. Therefore, He will live forever in us and we will live forever *with* Him.

He wants a continual turning to Him, and relying on Him, to reinforce what He desires; relationship between Father and daughter and Father and son.

But why do we have to keep ourselves constantly going back to Him to know that this is the truth?

Simple. The enemy throws so many distractions at us to make us focus on our perceived problems. Problems with timing. Problems with age. You've missed the boat. Your opportunity passed you by. You're too old now. Those dreams aren't for you anymore. Problems with all kinds of stuff that is about future; problems with money, problems with people, and problems with questions about life in general. What will happen tomorrow or ten years from now?! The distracting thoughts that exist, to avert your time and attention from God, are endless. You can never achieve peace, or victory, in taking on these questions about future provision and future questions yourself. Sufficient is the day with its issues and challenges. Let God have tomorrow. Outside of a personal relationship where you can find assurance, direction, and confidence in all these areas, your own fears and doubts will paralyze your forward motion.

No don't blank out and be stupid and not deal with a tomorrow problem if God is bringing it to you to deal with today. If God has a solution for tomorrow's problem, today, then deal with Him as He instructs that day.

In my alone time with the Lord, where my relationship is found, developed, and strengthened, I explode with His purposes, visions, and revelation. It's the most incredible state of being. When you're with God you're powerful beyond measure. He provides His strength. He provides His wisdom. He provides clarity and vision and direction. More than anything, He provides the ability to truly let go of our worries and trust in Him. Today. One day at a time.

From this place, I remember that He has plans for my life and that I am a daughter whose always provided for.

"For I know the plans I have for you" says the Lord. "They are plans for good and not for evil, to give you a sure future and a hope." **Jeremiah 29:11 (TLB)**

He knows the plans He has for you! They are not the current disasters and evil situations that may be plaguing you. They aren't the guys who hurt you. They aren't the sickness you've just been diagnosed with. Yes, Jesus warned us that in this world we would suffer tribulation, but God promises good plans for your future and plans that you ought to have tremendous hope in because no matter what you're going through He also said; fear not for I have overcome the world. He personally promises to lead you through it and complete the work He began in you.

Such glory, and so many answers, is found in fighting off distractions and spending quiet time alone with the Lord, growing in your personal relationship and knowledge of Him and who He is. As I look back over my life thus far, I see the amount of time that was lost in the war Satan waged with the weapons of distraction, pain, and brokenness. These obstacles steal the limited time we have on earth to walk in victory by keeping us from the source of our victory. Gods timing is everything, yet the myriad of distractions, and to do lists, that needlessly occupy us only serve to divert our lives from the fact that we have a limited amount of time here on earth to walk out our callings. This time is shortened day-by-day and moment-by-moment. It's time to get it right; because time is limited and *timing is everything*!

Christina Reynolds, an amazing worship leader at the International House of Prayer, IHOP, in Kansas City, asked me how I would say my ideal 'timing' and the lord's 'timing' differed on my journey so far; especially with gaining influence for the kingdom.

I realized the Lord gave me true revelation for this question when the answer came out of my mouth that day. Consequently, I had been in deep communion with God for hours the morning I received this question. I knew, when I answered her, that this was God speaking through me.

I think timing is something we can affect greatly! In general, I believe, as Charles Finney, that God's timing is now and always. Our timing doesn't line up with His when we don't line up with Him. His timing is always now and the answer is always yes. But, we are the problem.

We delay His timing because we are broken and fearful. We are lazy and lack dedication to seek Him daily, every moment dying to ourselves, living with our eyes and heart locked on Him and nothing else. Instead of trusting everything He says and walking in deep, deep, communion with Him, we trust in the works of our own manipulations and the perceived power of others.

My timing differed from His because, even though my timing was now and always also, I couldn't walk in His timing or mine because my life wasn't right. When we are not right in our dedication to Him, and to His purposes, truly seeking Him only, He cannot give us what *we* desire now, nor can He give us what *He* desires now to give us. We would be destroyed by our own spiritual immaturity, which causes an inability to handle material abundance, power, and responsibility, thus delaying Gods timing constantly.

Because, He loves us way to much to lose us and because He wants our eternity assured more than He even wants us to be used by Him for His glory, He will put off even the fulfillment of His own purposes in the timing He would prefer. So in His love and mercy He will allow delays to His desire for NOW and ALWAYS blessings upon us to make sure we are safe and right and ready to receive the tremendous blessings He has for us, and had for us all along.

So, He is always ready. His timing is always now. But He is sovereign and He knows the end at the beginning so His love determines what He will allow and do each day.

That's what I have learned looking back at it all. Yes, I do believe that at a point He will use someone else for His plans and purposes, especially when timing is critical. I also understand that God's timing often involves waiting because some plans and purposes require a season. But ultimately, I believe that like any loving parent He will try as hard as He can, and for as long as He can, to bless us with the very thing we want. Right now. Again, as long as it isn't bad for us, or will separate us from Him.

His promises are spoken in His word. But they are made real in your quiet time and in your personal relationship with Him. Because of this amazing truth, and the incredible power it holds, Satan wants us distracted, distant, and never motivated or interested in getting quiet and still before the Lord, spending time developing a relationship with Him. After all, God is still Satan's enemy. The battle is still between good and evil upon the earth. And, Satan never wanted to submit or surrender to God.

The question is; do you?!

26

ON THE THRONE

He says, "Be still, and know that I am God; I will be exalted among the nations, I will be exalted in the earth."
Psalm 46:10 (NIV)

As I cried a deep prayer alone, in my prison cell, that first night, I could finally do what the Bible said; be still and know that He was God. Him, not me. Him, not the things I was doing, to do what I didn't yet know, that only He could do. I had come so far to be locked in 'isolation' to receive the isolation I needed.

In a place where there is no stillness one simply cannot *know* that God is real. The stillness starts inside you. I believe that being still inside is easier for some than others. For many of us the slightest noises or distractions steal our focus from finding stillness inside. For others they can exist in an environment of utter chaos and noise and have the ability to be in a still place inside themselves. I am of the former type and Satan has a truly easy target with me.

Computers, phones, people, busyness, all easily grab my attention and create noise inside me. But more than anything, the voices that battled the thoughts and insecurities inside me were what had ruled for years. In a place where there is no stillness all that ever grows is chaos and confusion. I hadn't been still ever. I had been running and moving so fast for so long by my own devices or by the devices of others that I simply didn't know the God I thought I knew.

What I did know was that I was struck down to the lowest point imaginable. I was helpless, lacking any control at all, as if I ever had any, and in desperate need of a God who could provide supernatural intervention. In the stillness of my cell I learned the lessons of being real with God and myself. I had been blindly busy and distracted with one chief concern, so chief that it was my idol; me. There was so much of *me* that I was distracted with that I literally lost me in the noise and confusion...of *me*. Mostly, I lost the relationship that had begun tugging at my heart when River and I were together; the one I felt existed with Jesus.

In short, God wanted His proper place on the throne. He intended to be the only One exalted in my life. He wanted to answer my questions and talk to me. I needed answers. I needed a way out of the chaos involved with being me. Chaos that was inflicted by others and chaos that was inflicted by myself. I just didn't have the clarity, focus, or dedication to eliminate the noise and get still and get to know God. I was unable because of all my pain, and all that I was doing to numb my pain, to be still and know that God was God.

Be still and know *yourself* by knowing your *Creator*. Be still and know the plans He has for your life. Be still and know everything you need to know each day for your entire life.

I fought my way in my prison cell, as I fight my way daily, into the joy of the reality that God knows all things, and I too can know, from this place of stillness before Him. Satan has no choice but to flee from this place. There is no room for him there. In the stillness, I am no longer susceptible to his distracting thoughts. I am no longer a slave to fear. I am no longer unable to hear from my Father, rather I am able to hear clearly every word and every leading He has for me. This state of living deeply connected to God is a terrifying thing to the enemies of God; because it's where we win.

I want to win. Do you want to win?

Where do we win?

We win staying connected to Him.

27

WHERE IS HE

"Can a man hide himself in hiding places so I do not see him?" declares the LORD "Do I not fill the heavens and the earth?" declares the LORD. **Jeremiah 23:24 (NASB)**

So, once we are still where is He and how do we know that He is God?

Well that's easy. He's everywhere you are. He's certainly in the Bible.

How do you know Him? You read the Bible.

How do you learn that He is God? You watch the promises in the Bible play themselves out in your life.

As you begin to walk with Him and talk with Him and live for Him you begin to think like Him and see like Him and understand like Him. A glorious freedom and peace begin to accompany you everywhere you go.

Yes, but the Bible?

OK, for my friends who don't believe, yet feel compelled to read because you know me, love me, or are simply curious. I feel you bristling with doubt, unbelief, skepticism, criticism, and all kinds of preconceived notions and wounds inflicted by others who called themselves Christians. I know. I'm so sorry for my brothers and sisters in Christ who are immature in love, or knowledge of the word, and have said horrible things to you, and about you, in Jesus name. They are false Christians. And, He's as sick to his stomach as I am. But He is also as forgiving in His heart as we each need to be with each other because that is love at its highest. We all know, no matter what your faith or lack of faith dictates, that love is the highest expression of God in the universe.

So, let us try to reach higher, together, right now as we deal with the Bible.

The Bible is an incredibly, supernatural, book filled with things that can blow your mind, and will, if you give it an open minded read. Honestly, even if you don't give it an open minded read it will still blow your mind. Trust me.

But, you say you don't have time, or you don't understand what you're reading, or you're not sure it was really written by God because man probably added to it and took away from it so it can't be sane to fully depend on reading a book that's been tampered with by men. Oh and yes, I love this one; its outdated and irrelevant for a modern world such as the one you live in today.

And, the most compelling, important, resistance you have; I'm afraid to read it because deep inside I know it says my lifestyle is wrong and I don't want to feel condemned and judged and unloved because I disagree with that.

Les deal with these one by one.

You don't have time?

Easy. Then you don't have time to win. You don't have time to know if God, or His word, is real. You don't have time to know the plans God has for your life, if He is real. You don't have time to even understand how to achieve the plans you have for your own life. You don't have time for a relationship with God, who created you. You don't have time to know Him. You don't have time to know yourself.

Therefore, you don't have time to know how to fight the daily battles that come against you. You don't have time for breakthrough. You don't have time for success. You don't have time for love. You don't have time for knowledge or power. And, you don't have time for wisdom to live life and to live it more abundantly. You don't have time to walk in victory daily.

You. Don't. Have. Time.

What you do have is plenty time for losing!

Moving along to those of you *with* time.

Number two. You don't understand what you're reading?!

OK that's a legitimate one, but even so, it's easily remedied. Get a translation that you can understand.

When I first read the Bible I was given one called The Good News Bible. I actually like to call it the Bible for first graders. But, I could also call it the Bible that changed my life forever and set me on a course with my destined purposes in Christ. Because, I understood it. Glory Hallelujah.

That Bible translation was so simple for me to understand that for the first time in my life, I not only read the Word with comprehension, and clear understanding, I actually enjoyed it. Yes I said that.

What I didn't enjoy was being bored, and not understanding what I was reading. What I didn't enjoy was feeling like I couldn't tell anybody at all that I wasn't engaged, or able to enjoy, the book that everybody else was saying was a NY Times bestseller, and the most amazing, revolutionary, life-changing book of all time, if you follow me.

Because of being given a translation I could understand I was given deep and complicated revelation from God about my situation, my destiny, and myself. Because I could understand what I was reading I began to enjoy it, no crave it, in ways I had never experienced before with ANY book. Because, a dear sweet woman gave me a translation I could actually understand, I fell in love with the Word of God.

He wants to speak to us. He doesn't want to hide the ball from us and He surely doesn't want to confuse us and leave us feeling as if we must be the ones the Bible refers to when it refers to those whose eyes are blind and whose ears cannot hear. Once you've read and grown some you'll naturally require deeper study. You can then begin to read different translations of the same thing and add commentaries to your study so you're growing in a manner consistent with what God wants for you. He doesn't want us to stagnate. Stagnation leads to backsliding and falling into all kinds of situations and behavior a mature believer shouldn't be in.

After I was saved and had read through the Bible more than a couple times, I grew stagnant and ended up in Hollywood. Spiritual stagnation and Hollywood are a dangerous combination. More about that later.

Right now I love the, NLT, New Living Translation. It's simple and clear and written in really easy language to comprehend. I've read through an NIV, New International Version and the New King James. Let's be real, however, King James is tough if you're an average minded person, as I consider myself to be. My husband and son love it and prefer it. I like a simple translation that I can easily follow but I often check what I've read in another translation or in a King James. For even more revelation or understanding of a passage going to the Greek or Hebrew original words, meanings, and tenses opens up a whole world of original intent and discovery. This all comes, however, from initially reading, understanding, and enjoying the Word of God made alive in you.

OK if you're saying to yourself what are you talking about?   It gets clear when you see and do it for yourself.

There are some amazing tools today that nearly eliminate the excuse of not understanding the Bible. If you have a computer, or a phone with wifi or cell service, you can google Blue Letter Bible. To me, this is the best resource around for seeing various translations all in one place. There are a multitude of commentaries from some global heavyweights whose teachings and insights are amazing. My personal favorite is Chuck Smith, the founder of the Calvary Chapels worldwide. His commentaries are simple to understand, easy to follow, and filled with deep revelation about the Word of God in every chapter and verse in the Bible. There are even audio versions you can listen to, instead of read, if you're so inclined. It's all free. That's always the right price.

And, of course, you can always ask someone who knows much more than you do to explain the things you're reading in your Bible to you. Asking questions of someone whose studied more and is further along in their relationship with God and with Jesus is always smart. I may have the busiest day ever, but I will stop and take time from my day to answer, to the best of my ability, anybody who has a question about the Word of God. Register your email and send me an email directly at www.cynthiagarrett.org Most people love to teach when someone really wants to learn. Find a brother or sister in Christ and bug them with any and every question you have. Get your answers. That's my motto.

Next, I love number three! You say you're not sure the Bible is really accurate; that it's not really God's words because man probably added to it, and took away from it, therefore it can't be smart to fully believe what you read.

It's crazy how many people sit there day after day, year after year, in this place of unquestioned unbelief. They believe but they don't really believe. Or, they believe, but only the parts they feel good about believing. The parts that seem inconsistent with what they desire to be true, they just file away as something outdated, or something to put in the shadows of doubt where unbelief forms and strengthens itself. These people are content to literally avoid asking the deep questions and getting to the bottom of whether the Bible is really the inerrant and inspired word of God for fear they might have to change themselves completely, change their lives completely, or actually discover that God is not real. Is any one of these paradigms so small that it shouldn't be dealt with, or so big that it should be avoided?

NO!

I simply cannot understand this state of complete blissful ignorance! How can anyone justify not diving deeply into whatever you have to, in order to find out if a book that lays claim to as big a claim as the Bible does, is real or not? Your entire life, eternity, salvation, and family history depend on whether or not it's real. Whether you even accept that, or not, wouldn't you want proof beyond a reasonable doubt that it's real or not real? Wouldn't you want to be certain that your decision that the Bible is false, or even partially false, is absolutely correct? Or do you always make life decisions without thoroughly checking and understanding the facts upon which you base your claims?

My husband, started out an atheist. In the quest to prove God did not exist, he ended up proving God's existence to himself beyond a shadow of a doubt. He often muses on what life would have been like if he had stopped at his unbelief and never questioned whether he was factually justified or not. He lives with such a full relationship with Christ, and with such peace in all things, that I cannot imagine him any other way. Yet, it was his decision to be certain about the existence of God, or not, that have given him years of peace, and success, as well as the wisdom that causes many, many, people to depend on his guidance, his teachings, and his judgment. His entire destiny, and the destinies of thousands of people to come, lay in his doing the *work* to understand if there was a God and a risen Savior, named Jesus, who was God on earth in the flesh. He changed his entire life, and belief system, when he discovered that his atheism was nonsense and the nonsense that he thought was the Bible was actually more logical than his atheism.

My husband told me a story about a woman he knew who saw a snake and screamed and puller her shirt over her head so she couldn't see it anymore. As if her not seeing the snake actually made the snake less real. People can be this dumb. Since God didn't intentionally create fools one can only *choose* to be one. I trust that nobody wants to choose foolishness. However, to sit in a place of unquestioned unbelief, is as foolish as turning your back on the things you don't understand, or aren't sure of, hoping that ignorance will actually be an acceptable belief system on judgment day.

It certainly won't be an acceptable excuse to yourself when you realize how much life you've been robbed of once you discover that the Bible actually *is* real. It has been proven by science, by scholars, by archaeology, and by time, to be the inerrant Word of God. It has tested out in more ways than it has yet to still test out.

The research exists and the people exist who can answer your questions. I can promise you that every question you have or have thought in the back of your mind, about whether the Bible was really

Gods accurate word, I've asked and found answers for also. It is real. The Bible is real. It's bigger than your questions. It's bigger than the questions of everyone around you who causes you to question. It's bigger than your doubts and fears. It's sixty-six books, written over two thousand years, by over forty men, and every word lines up. Even if you see what you think is an inconsistency somewhere, ask someone who knows it well. It lines up.

Translating from original Greek and Hebrew texts into English can cause what appear to be inconsistencies as well, but that's why you have to know how to study the Bible, and cross reference the things you read, from time to time. You need this personal knowledge and skill in your tool belt to satisfactorily combat the lies that war against your faith trying to steal the truth little by little.

Scholar, RT Kendall, wrote an article recently for Charisma magazine. He called it perhaps the most important thing he will have ever written. That's a huge statement from an 80 year old scholar of the Word whose lived his life in pursuit of an accurate and full understanding of the entire counsel of God and written over 60 books. His statement in this article was a simple, yet harsh, indictment of the body of Christ.

He simply said...Christians today don't read their Bibles!

He stated frankly that there are pastors leading flocks, and people teaching sermons, and they're not reading their Bibles, the way they should, if at all. This is scary, but I too have found it to be true. I've met men and women leading large groups and churches who don't know the word of God. My twenty-four year old son, and certainly my husband, is way more knowledgeable than many pastors. People look to leaders to be able to answer questions, or show them the way to an answer. For what it's worth, I want to issue a loud cry of agreement with Dr. Kendall that it's time to wake up and read our Bibles.

And, next you say, you can't believe because the Bible is outdated and irrelevant for a modern world such as the one you live in today.

Well...

"Jesus Christ is the same yesterday, today, and forever."
Hebrews 13:8 (NIV)

I'm tempted to drop the mic on this scriptural statement.

It pretty in your face. He's the same. Yesterday. Today. Forever. He doesn't change, hasn't changed, and won't change. You can call on Him and trust Him in exactly the same way the apostles who hung with Him did. If you apply anything you read to your life today, not only will you find the greatest knowledge and wisdom for any and all situations and issues; you will find freedom for your heart, vision for your endeavors, and peace for your mind. The same things He provided when He walked the earth.

He is still the way to the Father. He is still resurrected from the dead and alive in us through the Holy Spirit. He is still the One who came to bind up the broken hearted and to set the captives free. He is the same. Yesterday. Today. And, Forever.

And, lastly, you say you're simply afraid to read the Bible!

This is the most compelling, important, resistance you can actually have. You say, "I'm afraid to read it because deep inside I know it may say that my lifestyle is wrong, or the way that I think is wrong, or the things that I desire are wrong." And, frankly, you don't want to feel condemned, judged, and unloved because you disagree with what you read, or cannot figure out how to be what you read, or live in a manner consistent with what you may read. So, you'd rather not read it at all. Because, you are scared. So was I. So am I still...but...

Such love has no fear, because perfect love expels all fear. If we are afraid, it is for fear of punishment, and this shows that we have not fully experienced his perfect love.
1 John 4:18 (NLT)

Much can be said about letting your fears stop you from anything. But, even more can be said about love overcoming your fears. You see, you are loved by God. In whatever lifestyle you're currently living. In whatever way your mind currently thinks. With whatever desires you may or may not have; you are created to be a child of God.

And, God loves you.

Avoiding Him, and the reality of Him, or the existence of Him, won't change the fact that He is real and that He created you to *love* you and take care of you. He wants to walk with you and talk with you and help you overcome your deepest fears and your darkest pains. Your lifestyle is no surprise to Him. Your desires don't shock Him or even offend Him. And, your way of thinking doesn't put Him off. He loves you. He desires for you to love Him in return. He desires for you to know Him in return. And, He desires for you to walk with Him through all things. He loves you. Start there. The required changes are between you and Him and I can promise you this; He won't change anything you don't want changed. He won't take anything you don't want taken.   And, He won't remove any desire you truly desire to hold on to. His love is perfect. And there is no fear in perfect love.

Your fears are all concerning punishment. He wants to introduce you to perfect love, not perfect punishment. Perfect love invites all of us to Him. All of us come as we are. All of us leave better. He loves us.

28

SAVED BY GRACE

Now there was a man of the Pharisees named Nicodemus, a ruler of the Jews. This man came to Jesus by night and said to him, "Rabbi, we know that you are a teacher come from God, for no one can do these signs that you do unless God is with him." Jesus answered him, "Truly, truly, I say to you, unless one is born again he cannot see the kingdom of God." Nicodemus said to him, "How can a man be born when he is old? Can he enter a second time into his mother's womb and be born?" Jesus answered, "Truly, truly, I say to you, unless one is born of water and the Spirit, he cannot enter the kingdom of God. That which is born of the flesh is flesh, and that which is born of the Spirit is spirit. Do not marvel that I said to you, 'You must be born again.' The wind blows where it wishes, and you hear its sound, but you do not know where it comes from or where it goes. So it is with everyone who is born of the Spirit."

Nicodemus said to him, "How can these things be?" Jesus answered him, "Are you the teacher of Israel and yet you do not understand these things? Truly, truly, I say to you, we speak of what we know, and bear witness to what we have seen, but you do not receive our testimony. If I have told you earthly things and you do not believe, how can you believe if I tell you heavenly things? No one has ascended into heaven except he who descended from heaven, the Son of Man. And as Moses lifted up the serpent in the wilderness, so must the Son of Man be lifted up, that whoever believes in him may have eternal life.

For God so loved the world that he gave his only begotten Son, that whoever believes in him should not perish but have eternal life. For God did not send his Son into the world to condemn the world, but in order that the world might be saved through him. Whoever believes in him is

not condemned, but whoever does not believe is condemned already, because he has not believed in the name of the only Son of God. And this is the judgment: the light has come into the world, and people loved the darkness rather than the light because their works were evil. For everyone who does wicked things hates the light and does not come to the light, lest his works should be exposed. But whoever does what is true comes to the light, so that it may be clearly seen that his works have been carried out in God."
John 3:1-21 (NASB)

In my, cold, stone, cell that first or second night I had a dream that was so vivid it has marked my life forever. I will never forget it.

I dreamt that I was talking to a woman who I thought could be my grandmother, who was in heaven, because she looked exactly like her, but at the same time I realized that she was an angel. She was standing on what appeared to be a white puffy bed of clouds. She was dressed all in white from head to toe including a covering over her head. She wore what looked like a 'habit' worn by the nuns I went to Catholic school with, as a little girl. She held out a book to me that was in her hand and on it was written the words 'Good News.'

"Do you know what this is?" She asked me.
I was puzzled. I wasn't sure of the answer. So, I just stared at her taking it all in.
Then she answered saying, "This is God's word. If you read it and devote your life to it. It will change your life. He will save you."
As I reached out to her to take it I was back to sleep. The dream ended or the vision ended. I'm still not clear. All I know is that it was as real to me as the sun shining.

The next morning, completely unsure as to what my day, or my life, was going to look like I woke up when I heard someone put food inside the room. They placed a tray in the room and nodded curiously at me, the strange new inmate, before leaving. I decided to turn on the TV that was hanging on the wall. At least it could keep me company while I ate. The TV news was filled with images of...me. I sat stunned. This was notoriety not fame. This was not what I had dreamt of since childhood. Yet, there I was plastered all across every TV channel. Images of me with my head low, crying, being escorted by Carabinieri, police, into the prison

I actually found the food wasn't awful at all. In the three months I would be there I ate well. I ate. Which was possibly a blessing in itself because I hadn't eaten much at all for many months prior.
As I was finishing my meal, a woman, whose name was Signora Mariucha, came to open my cell door. I was behind the bars but she stood with the open solid door smiling curiously at me.

We would through the next few months develop a beautiful friendship and a lasting respect. I will forever be grateful to her for seeing, in my eyes, the condition of my heart, and the innocence in my soul. When we would be able to finally communicate fully, in Italian, we would have amazing conversations together about life. She had daughters my age; the age of so many of the girls in prison. I think being a mother gave her a much deeper awareness and sensitivity to us girls. She seemed to have wisdom about what issues drove many of us to end up in here. I, for one, had been accepting so much less than what God had for me. Signora Mariucha always showed me love and understanding. Because of her presence, this prison was actually a lot like living in a really difficult house, but with a really beautiful mother.

She walked away momentarily and opened the cell door of the room next to me and said something to the two girls inside that I would discover were sisters. The younger one, who was tiny in size and stature, came out and stood next to her at my door. Her name was Rita. She looked at me curiously, but not really directly, in the eyes. Her head was mostly down and her gaze averted almost as if she walked in complete shame. My heart went out to her immediately because she seemed so young, so afraid, and so hopeless. Mariucha, had gotten an English Italian dictionary from the Marshall in the front office. Rita, who spoke very broken English, seemed happy to try and interpret and communicate with me. I would learn that Rita desired one thing, almost more than her freedom, and that was to learn to speak English. She loved Beatles songs. In my time there, I would translate Beatles songs for her, writing down the words in English, and she in exchange, would teach me Italian. Between the two of them that day, they explained that someone was coming to see me.

See me? I thought.

The three of us stood there finding words in the dictionary to communicate with each other. We looked up when we heard the sound of footsteps in the distance. They were rapidly approaching and possessed a quick clip that would best describe the person to whom they belonged; busy. Places to go. People to see and people to help. That is Suora Angela Niccoli.

As I looked down the long, cold, corridor that ran the length of the row of cells, I saw a woman dressed all in white, including a covering over her head. In her hand she was holding a book. As she got closer to me, I couldn't help but notice she bore a striking resemblance to my grandmother and to the angel that had appeared to me in my dream the night before!

She held out the book to me and said in Italian "hello I have something for you. Do you know what this is? This is Gods word. If you read it and devote your life to it He will save you!" I looked at Rita as she thrust the book at me to translate. I was in shock. I looked down at the book in the hands of this energetic little nun, who wore an all white traditional habit; the kind I hadn't seen since my childhood days in Catholic school. It covered her head. Across the cover, in big bold letters, was written the words Good News Bible.

Having never encountered a miracle before I gasped, burst into tears, and felt as if I would faint. My knees buckled. I was punched in the stomach with an amazing and powerful thrust. There would never be any mistaking the fact that *this* was indeed a miracle from God.

I would discover that Suora means nun in Italian. Angela, means angel.

I could not communicate with them, at this point in my journey, about why Suora Angela's appearance caused such a reaction in me. Over the months that it would take, after I became fluent in Italian, I would have many things to explain. I would share many experiences, many miracles, signs, and wonders with them; and especially with Suora Angela.

Suora Angela was my angel, who looked like my grandmother, who brought me the good news, and with whom I have remained close friends for many years. She was sent by God to bring me His Word. He was alive. He was real. He saw everything I was going through. He knew exactly where I was. And, He moved the earth and sent me a dream, and a vision, and an angel, so I would never doubt that God is real, He sees us and our struggles, and He alone saves souls, heals the broken hearted, transforms lives, and brings complete and total restoration and restitution for all that the enemy steals from our lives. He does all this through Jesus Christ. In the many questions I had asked God through the prior years of my life, about whether Jesus was indeed the only way to the Father, I would never need to ask again. *This* miracle was centered all around Jesus.

The Good News Bible that I was given was only The New Testament. Oddly enough, Suora Angela tried and tried she explained, to find an English translation of the entire Bible, but all she could find in English was The New Testament. I would laugh for hours when she explained this to me. Only God knew the depth of my confusion living in my new age dazed and confused, beloved California. This was his punctuation point on the answer to my questions about whether Jesus was indeed the way and the One.

I had read everything from, The Autobiography of a Yogi, by Paramahansa Yogananda, to the Quran, and its teachings about the Muslim faith. I had read new age books, science of the mind books, and the power of us as God books. I had gone into sweat lodges in Native American Indian rituals, and sat down with psychics, psychic artists, and spiritual healers. Yet, when I called out to God, at the end of my own rope, to know the real truth of who He was and what He wanted me to know; His answer was Jesus. And, to be certain I couldn't get confused, the only translation in English on the island was one for The New Testament. Point made. Point taken. There was no doubt that I would devote my life to this, even if my life would be spent in a prison cell.

The craziest thing I discovered over those few months is that while I was indeed in prison, locked up, without the freedom to do what I wanted, I had never been freer in my life. As I read the Word and God spoke and moved in it, and through it, in me and through me, I began being set free in ways that were beyond transformative. Victory and freedom were mine as I journeyed further into the Bible and all its promises and teachings. Even while physically imprisoned I was no longer in jail. I was having the greatest, most deeply personal, spiritual awakening of my life.

I gave my life to Christ, alone, in my cell. I remember the tears of joy, relief, epiphany, and emotional freedom I felt in that moment. I

165

experienced what I now knew, people meant, when they said they were 'born again.' I literally felt new, fresh, and childlike. I was alive with hope. I felt personally known and understood, for the very first time in my life, as I came to personally know and understand God.

Confusion cleared away and clarity settled in. What I couldn't understand I felt peace to give to Him, and what I could understand I felt relief to have been given answers for. I began to live in the moment for the first time in my life. My past was no longer controlling me in the same way, and my future was no longer something I felt the need to control. I chose to trust God with my life and I no longer worried about how I would get home, when I would get home, or if I would get home. I knew God *wanted* me to get home, so I trusted Him with the how's and when's.

29

BUONCAMMINO PRISON

Continue to remember those in prison as if you were together with them in prison, and those who are mistreated as if you yourselves were suffering
Hebrews 13:3 (NIV)

After the first few weeks, I was eventually moved from isolation where I had been in a cell alone, which I didn't mind at all, because I liked the privacy of my own space. I could pray freely, cry freely, and laugh freely. I had surrounded myself with people for so long, having always been in the center of the crowd that was running things socially, that I never had time alone to hear myself think, much less pray and talk to God.

That said, I was put into a larger cell, with Rita and Marilena, the two sisters whom I had befriended from the cell next door. The three of us were moved in with two other girls; one was a prostitute and one was caught running guns and drugs through the airport with her boyfriend. The two new girls were completely the opposite of Rita and Marilena. As kind as the two sisters were, these two girls were filled with a curious envy where I was concerned. I often felt a mean spiritedness directed toward me even though I couldn't really understand their Italian dialect very well.

I prayed and asked God to give me a quick and easy ability to understand and to speak the language. Having always been a communicator I needed to learn to communicate. I was compelled to learn Italian. I stepped up Rita's lessons with my English Italian dictionary and by asking tons of questions. However, I spent most of my time in the word, not studying Italian, so I honestly believe God simply gave me the supernatural ability to speak Italian that I had asked for.

I actually began learning the dialect before proper Italian and my attorney looked at me one day in horror and said, "No, Cinzia, you must learn the correct Italian. Oh my GOD!" The horrific expression on his face, that I would learn a dialect from this island in the south, was actually very funny. Rita complied and our lessons included only proper Italian, but with some knowledge of the dialect called, Sardo, because, as I was on their island, I felt I should understand both. People still find this hilarious.

I ventured out into the courtyard a few times with Rita and Marilena but there was an energy I didn't like outside amongst the other girls. As with our two new cellmates, I felt an odd sense of jealousy and resentment because of the amount of attention I received in the press and from the guards in the prison.

I think the prison staff, which dealt with those of us inside on a daily basis, knew I wasn't guilty of what I was being accused of. Therefore they treated me as well as possible inside a stone prison. This, did however, create additional animosity, when coupled with my constant star status on TV, as the daughter of a wealthy American businessman with ties to Hollywood and a rock star for a brother. Oh brother. Italians never cease to shy away from gross exaggerations, drama, and glamour. However, for some reason, they all felt sympathy for me. Not that I wasn't an extremely sympathetic character, because I certainly was. I had nobody close, I was thousands of miles from home, and the prosecutor was trying to give me twenty years for international drug trafficking!

In the Italian culture courting for years, prior to marriage, was the norm. People didn't approach marriage as cavalierly as I certainly had. My western culture had made me cavalier about everything. But, for an Italian to run off and marry someone after knowing him or her only three months, was absurd. They had deep compassion for me, probably understanding far more than I did about the man I married, who was on the other side of the prison with the men. But, they had to have found me to be incredibly naïve, at best. Stupid at worst.

The months there were very bizarre as it concerned Miloj and me. He sent an unending stream of letters and notes through whatever underground system of prison communication they all understood that I didn't. Girls I didn't know would walk by me and stick his letters in my hand or on my food tray, not realizing that I didn't want them. They couldn't read what he was writing me on the backs of all the pieces of paper and napkins so they had no idea that his communications were disturbing in the deepest of ways and that for me I wanted nothing more of them.

He would write love letters professing his undying love and devotion to me and his desire that I wouldn't leave him. Then there would be a letter threatening to cut my throat from ear to ear if I gave any information against him. He even wrote a letter one day, with what he called a self-portrait in it, that was the most disturbing thing I'd ever seen; it was a demon behind bars. Almost cartoon like; it was the creepiest thing to actually look at. I can still see the eyes of the thing in my mind till this day. It was part of a letter which went so many directions emotionally I finally began to understand the levels of deep criminal psychoses and pathology he operated in. More than anything, I felt the most bizarre terror when I realized that he had drawn a picture of a demon I had seen before; the one that manifested in front of me in the guy who had come to my apartment at three-o-clock in the morning to bring me drugs. I remember staring for a long time at the picture realizing once again the inescapable reality that spiritual warfare is real.

I would see this demon once again many years later while visiting a girlfriend in California, who happened to have a friend in town from England. Her friend called herself a psychic artist and she wanted to draw a picture of my spirit guide to bless me. I reluctantly allowed her too, not wanting to be rude. When she presented me the drawing, after having set quietly drawing for nearly twenty minutes I stared at the picture in shock. It was the image of the same demon yet again. She smiled, so pleased as she told me it was my spirit guide and that he looked out for me. She wanted me to place it under my bed for protection. Once I connected the dots, I knew she was incredibly deceived and tapping into the demonic realm. Since she wasn't interested in a conversation with me about why God says do not consult spirits; much less about Jesus Christ, it became clear she was being used to try and bring some demonic spiritual confusion back into my life. This experience is one of many that have taught me the truth of 2 Timothy.

They will act religious, but they will reject the power that could make them godly. Stay away from people like that!
2 Timothy 3:5 (NLT)

Needless to say, I ran away from the demon when he showed up with that same mocking smile in my apartment and I knew not to entertain Miloj's letters when the demon showed up with that same mocking smile in a photo Miloj called a self portrait.   I also knew, once again, to stay away from this lovely, yet confused, English woman who was actively tapping into the demonic and giving people guidance spiritually that was powerless in the least and utterly destructive at best.

In the beginning week or so I had two attorneys who were court appointed, who showed up regularly. They informed me, after a number of days, that my mother had been reached and that the consulate would visit me soon. I felt a rush of relief being told that my mom at least now knew where I was and that I was alive. A week or two would pass before I was to hear her voice on a phone, however. Miloj wrote repeatedly to get rid of the two court appointed men because they had no power he would write in his letters. He would tell me to get someone with a name that knew drugs. I would always sit wondering whether he was nuts. I didn't need someone who knew drugs, in my mind, because I was innocent. Miloj was the guilty one. The two public defenders in my case, however, couldn't speak English and were quickly replaced by an attorney from Milan who did, that my family hired. Mirko, was young and charismatic and probably never should have taken my case because he didn't have the connections to the island to understand what would have likely sent me home in a few weeks versus the nearly two years I would spend fighting. However, he was like oxygen to me throughout the immediate months to come.

Mirko, was a blessing in that I needed someone in those early days who could get me through the actual fear of Miloj that I had, and help me shed my guilt of abandoning another human being that Miloj exploited constantly. I was afraid he would kill me as some of his letters said he would. I was afraid he would send people to my mom's home to kill her as some of his letters said. After a month inside, when I found out I was pregnant, I was afraid he would have my baby kidnapped as some of his letters also said he would. He tried every threat imaginable to get me to not go against him in trial, to pay for his attorneys, and to make my attorneys defend him also.

Then, when fear didn't seem to be enough, he would tell me how God would be mad at me and hate me if I went against my husband. He played on my faith and my desire to always do the right thing, using my strengths as weapons against me.

"Now is time to prove you are really woman who loves God. You do what husband says and God is happy." Manipulations and lies and deceit; It just kept coming. He simply didn't want to be separated from me because he needed to control me.

Mirko, had some conversations with Miloj early on because he didn't understand if he was to actually represent us both. He wanted to understand if it would be beneficial to me. Mirko knew that he was retained by my family; Lenny to be exact. But, Miloj kept insisting to Mirko that, of course, he was to be included in my legal defense and that he would tell the truth and help me if Mirko made my family help him.

One afternoon, while seated alone together, in the stone room designated for his meetings with me, Mirko finally looked at me square in the eyes. He spoke the last words I ever needed to hear about Miloj Badovic.

"Cinzia, you are like a baby. You don't understand a thing. Do you know this man you marry is the worst kind of dog I have ever seen in my life? He absolutely does not love you! Do you know he tried to blame this problem on you when you were in the interrogations for two days after your arrest? He wants to keep you and your family involved with him so he can use you. I say this to you because you need to know. I don't want to defend him or to help him. He is a piece of s*t and he's trying to put you in s*t! He goes regularly to *Turkey*! Do you know what would happen to you if he took you to Turkey instead of here in Cagliari? You stay entire life in prison or they sentence you to death. He does not love you! I think he marry you just for passport because American passport is valuable to him. You have to wake up. I understand you read the Bible and it's good but this is not God who do this to you. You are good person, but stupid girl. Tell me please, what kind of animal put his *wife* in a mess like this?"

I sat there speechless, perfectly understanding his English, even with his Italian accent. I felt my chest rise and fall and I heard my own breathing. I got it. I knew he was right. I had suspected it all along. But, I suppose hearing it from a complete stranger solidified that the end of the road had been reached, for this guy and for me, long before we ever met. I failed. This was not redeemable. I had to accept a total failure of myself and move forward for myself.

I lived in a daze my first few weeks in prison. So much information was coming at me; from the police, the attorneys, the news, the newspapers, and God. I felt as if I had to listen deeply in spirit every day so as not to miss any divine directions for all that I was processing. I suppose the greatest instruction I got was the one that kept telling me not to take the Valium, and whatever other pills I was being given daily to keep me calm, because I was pregnant.

30

CHRISTIAN

Women, however, will be saved through childbearing, if they continue in faith, love, and holiness, with self-control
1 Timothy 2:15 (BSN)

My pregnancy was quite simply the miracle out of left field that nobody, not even me, really expected. I was negative in every pregnancy test when I was processed in a month prior, and Miloj and I hadn't really been sleeping together much with all the chaos of Paris. He just wasn't interested. I was usually too distraught, disgusted, or dismayed to have sex with my new husband anyway. On top of the fact of my situation with my husband was also the doctor who informed me, a couple years prior, that I would have a hard time conceiving, absent a lot of medical intervention. I had a myriad of female issues from the day I began menstruating and there was little expectation, certainly by my gynecologist then, that I would have kids.

After the first couple weeks in jail I stopped swallowing the pills, Valium or Adavan I suspect, that I was given twice daily to keep me calm. God began telling me in my Spirit to stop taking them so I listened. I would keep them under my tongue, till the medics left, and then spit them back in the cup and pass them through the window bars, of my room, over to the window next door, for Rita and Marilena to have. As we neared Christmas, I experienced a couple mornings of light nausea, and again, I felt the Spirit urging me to ask for another pregnancy test. So, I did.

I was learning to trust my instincts, my gut, and my sixth sense. Many people call it many things; except what it quite seriously needs to be looked at as. I had called it so many things and certainly never listened. But, my growing new relationship with Jesus was teaching me that these leadings and promptings deep inside were something serious to always be prayed about, as it could likely be God trying to inform me of what actions to take or not take. There was no hocus pocus, inner sixth sense that I controlled, as the world wants us to think, so God isn't recognized. There was God and the fact that as scripture says;

For in him we live, and move, and have our being; as certain also of your own poets have said, for we are also his offspring
Acts 17:28 (KJV)

The Holy Spirit of the living God now lived inside me. When I was born again the Holy Spirit, was my gift in that prison cell. I was filled with Him. As a child, once this occurs, we are now lead of the Holy Spirit into all truth and wisdom. Sadly, this is the most misunderstood aspect of God.

And I will ask the Father, and he will give you another advocate to help you and be with you forever; the Spirit of truth. The world cannot accept him, because it neither sees him nor knows him. But you know him, for he lives with you and will be in you. I will not leave you as orphans; I will come to you.
John 14: 16-18 (NIV)

God loved me. He had gone to some great lengths to get my attention, speak to me, and get me His word, telling me carefully to live my life by it. So, I had no doubt that He was speaking to me constantly and leading me, through His word, and through the Holy Spirit of truth that lived in me. I knew He was telling me a miracle was in the making inside me.

A couple days before Christmas Eve, Mariucha, gave me another pregnancy test at my insistence. I don't really know if she was supposed to or had permission from the judge to; but she did. On Christmas Eve, breaking protocol, she joyfully came to my cell to tell me that it was positive and to stay calm now for my baby. We cried tears of joy.

When she left I sat on my bunk, hands on my very flat tummy, in awe. I was 25 pounds underweight, for my five foot ten inch frame, had been in severe shock and mental anguish for weeks, and consumed a diet of cocaine and alcohol for nearly six months. Yet, I was pregnant. There was a baby growing inside me. All I could do was hold my stomach and cry tears of gratitude. I was deeply, deeply, aware that this child was the miracle referred to by the scripture I had read in the car that fateful night racing through the south of France.

No temptation has overtaken you except what is common to mankind. And God is faithful; he will not let you be tempted beyond what you can bear. But when you are tempted, he will also provide a way out so that you can endure it.
1 Corinthians 10:13 (NIV)

At the moment I was told that I was pregnant, I did not know that this baby would be my way out of my immediate mess, because of the pregnancy law that had to be invoked, but my son, Christian, would serve to be a constant way out of darkness and chaos into a light that grows brighter, day by day, until this very moment. He has been the gift of my salvation.

It's odd, but one of the many miracles I recognize in this experience is the fact that, I never connected this moment and my child to Miloj at all. It's as if, from day one, God gave me something with this pregnancy that was always only intended to be for *me*. Even my relationship with my son today has never been influenced by any need

176

to know or seek out his biological father. He's never been interested, even though I've given him the facts of his birth, including his father's name. We've just always been protected by God to find sufficiency in each other, until the day Roger appeared and, where others failed, I knew that he was the one to correctly be called Christian's father.

While I may have chosen incorrectly again, if I only had myself to care for, my love and devotion to my son would never allow me to choose incorrectly for him. I preferred to remain alone, or live in sin, versus marry the wrong man *ever* again.

Mirko was able to apply a law that, absent terrorist activity, prohibited me from being held in a cell, due to my pregnancy. All I needed was to successfully reach my third month of pregnancy and have an address in Cagliari. So, my mom came over to find the Residence Ulivi e Palme. It would be my home once released. She found a really cute studio apartment with a balcony for me to live in while under house arrest. My release date turned out to be my birthday, February 16th.

On my release day, when I finally met my mom in the front office, relief swept through my veins replacing blood. I was so happy to see her. I was processed out and escorted to the Residence and while it was amazing I had a horrible, dark, scary secret I needed to share with my mom but couldn't. People surrounded us all day that day. Police escorts and Carabinieri monitored my movement from my cell to the main office to the car and into the residence apartment where I would remain throughout the trial.

Once at the residence, inside the place I would call home, I was finally able to speak to her and I erupted in tears.
"Mom, I don't know if I've lost the baby or not!"
"What?" She stammered.

I explained to her that I had hoped and prayed, for weeks, that Christian was still growing inside me after nearly three months of hiding from everyone that I had been bleeding. My body started attempting a miscarriage; a few days after Mariucha told me I was indeed pregnant. I felt from the Spirit, that if I said anything they would immediately do a DNC and remove the pregnancy. It would have been far less complicated for them legally to deal with me if my baby was gone and I knew it. The fact that I was pregnant was a huge saving grace to me that the prosecutor did not like. The only thing that kept me standing with a shred of faith that I had not silently miscarried was that I had another dream that I knew was from God.

In my dream, A few weeks prior, I was rummaging through a box. It was filled with baby clothes. Written on the chest of a newborn's onesie was the phrase 2 Corinthians 6. When I woke up in my cell I knew it was scripture that I hadn't yet read. So I opened my Bible to see if there was such a scripture. I found that there was. This is what it said:

In our work together with God, then, we beg you who have received God's grace not to let it be wasted. Hear what God says:

"When the time came for me to show you favor,
*   I heard you;*
when the day arrived for me to save you,
*   I helped you."*
Listen! This is the hour to receive God's favor; today is the day to be saved!
2 Corinthians 6:1-2 (GNB)

Tears of joy streamed down my face, in my lower bunk, as I was flooded with His peace. No matter what the enemy said to me to make me believe my baby was dead I would not receive it. I did not receive it. God had spoken again, in my dreams, and I had no doubt what He was saying. This child would save me, even as I was being saved by Him, and my acceptance of Him, as my Savior. I held my tongue and laid in bed for the remaining two months I was in prison. I felt the Holy Spirit was telling me to just rest and read the Word and that's basically all I did.

It felt so good to share the weight of this secret burden with her. My mother reassured me that everything would be ok, and that sometimes breakthrough bleeding or spotting occurs. I told her about the dream I had about the scripture written on the baby clothes and I felt His peace again, even as I shared the experience with her. I still experienced some further relief, peace, and excitement when my stomach finally protruded, in my fifth month, and an ultrasound revealed a healthy heartbeat and a normally developing fetus.

The next blessing, far less important yet equally significant in terms of our eventual freedom, was that somehow, someway, my passport which was confiscated when I was arrested, had been knowingly or unknowingly, given to me in a pile with all my things, when I was released from the prison. This oversight, or divine blessing, as I knew it was, still baffles everyone ever involved in my story. Standard protocol would never have permitted my passport be returned to me while pending trials and a possible conviction.

Mirko shared all of this with us in the first months. He was so able to get through to me in those crucial initial weeks of my case, that my challenge from those days forward was not making him my savior, and wrapping myself up in him completely for protection and direction. I'm sure my sense of needing him clouded my judgment at times in my case. But, I learned as I read the Bible and prayed, that I had always been looking for a savior in the form of a man and God had provided the only one I ever needed already. He wanted me to cling to Him alone.

This growing knowledge of Jesus, as my ultimate helper, would finally push me to bring in another attorney, after a year of a legal mess in which I was convicted and sentenced to five and a half years. We requested an appeal, and hired a new attorney, who was very well known and connected on the island. His name was Professor Luigi Concas. He was a man with an educated and booming voice, a stern deliverance, and a heart inside that I was sure was made of gold. I saw it in his eyes, even though understanding his Italian and the legalese he used was difficult for me. Much more of a powerful father than a sexy hotshot, as Mirko was, he was able to achieve the fewer restrictions, based on my well publicized good behavior, that allowed me to finally have a loophole to attempt to leave Italy a year later; with my passport and my son in hand.

31

THE ESCAPE

So Peter was kept in prison, but the church was earnestly praying to God for him. The night before Herod was to bring him to trial, Peter was sleeping between two soldiers, bound with two chains, and sentries stood guard at the entrance. Suddenly an angel of the Lord appeared and a light shone in the cell. He struck Peter on the side and woke him up. "Quick, get up!" he said, and the chains fell off Peter's wrists.
Then the angel said to him, "Put on your clothes and sandals." And Peter did so. "Wrap your cloak around you and follow me," the angel told him. Peter followed him out of the prison, but he had no idea that what the angel was doing was really happening; he thought he was seeing a vision. They passed the first and second guards and came to the iron gate leading to the city. It opened for them by itself, and they went through it. When they had walked the length of one street, suddenly the angel left him.
Then Peter came to himself and said, "Now I know without a doubt that the Lord has sent his angel and rescued me from Herod's clutches and from everything they were hoping would happen."
Acts 12:5-11 (NIV)

Even in the fact of Italy's compassionate civility with their pregnancy law, I knew the series of very fortunate, and necessary, events that contributed to my eventual freedom was all God's hand; the angel He sent me so that I would be saved, my pregnancy, my passport, my status changes that gave me more and more unrestricted movement. A myriad of small miracles worked together for the greater miracle at work; my escape home to California. Knowing Him, I followed the miracles.

Prof. Concas explained to me, after the second appeals court upheld my sentence, that although he had requested an appeal to the Supreme Court, I would likely be given a hard choice by them once they ruled on my case six months later.

So, after nearly two years of fighting in vain, I could serve five and a half years in a prison in Rome, for women with babies, or give my son to my mother and serve my time without him. Prof. Concas was certain these would be my options. Neither of these, however, was an option I could bear to consider. The thought of missing the first five and a half years of my son's life brought me to a truly sad and dark place inside.

I left Prof. Concas' office with my mother that day. We were both distraught beyond belief. However, I knew that God had not given me this child as a temporary solution to jail, but as a permanent solution for anchoring the rest of my life. We would not be separated by the attack against *me*; we would be guided by the grace that birthed *him*.

I went into deep prayer for hours and hours through the night and into the next day. When the Lord finally spoke to me I knew what we were to do. We would check in with the police the following day, Thursday. This is what Prof. Concas obtained as the new requirement of my detention, pending our Supreme Court appeal. I would no longer be under house arrest with a need to be inside by nightfall. Now, every Thursday I would have to sign in at the police station. That Thursday, I felt The Lord say that we would sign in, and then leave for Milan. We would say we were traveling there so I could possibly get work, from Lenny's booking agent, while awaiting my next trial date in six months.

With the documents written as they were, I could explain that I would travel back to the island every Thursday to sign is as instructed by the judge. If stopped and detained my document stated that I was required to do this. However, if questioned, the document would probably not withstand the scrutiny of allowing me to move about the entire country. So if pressed, my loophole would likely be seen as an attempted escape landing me back in prison to await my Supreme Court appeal.

What the document did not say was that I had permission to leave Cagliari. Where it was silent we had a single opening. We also knew we had my passport which had not ever been restricted, according to the US Consulate. They recommended I leave Italy a year prior but I was intent to prove my innocence. My passport would hopefully get me across a border if I could get to one.

As I sat on my bed, in the studio apartment I had lived in for over a year and a half, I prayed and read the word and listened deep in my Spirit for God's instructions. Finally, He directed me to the book of Acts.

When I read the account of Peter walking out of prison, without any resistance, and how the prison doors opened, and the shackles fell off his hands and feet, I heard the Spirit say clearly to me; GO!!! It was time. And in God's mercy, I think He knew, that my mother couldn't handle draining another six months of financial resources, only to see me go to prison at the end of it; with or without my son.
"Mom, we are leaving." I stated with clear and final resolve.
"I would have to agree. But how?'" She asked, not quite understanding, but knowing, that I was hearing from God.
"I don't know yet. But, God does."

As soon as I was resolved, and knew that the Lord was with us, the ride to the ship appeared, in the form of a man I had befriended, who frequented the residence when he was in town for work. He volunteered to drive us to the ship saying we would look like a family husband, wife, child, and mother-in-law. It made sense. The only way off the island was the overnight ship and we would need to get a cabin for me to stay in and not draw attention to myself.

Barring a few curious looks, from people who clearly recognized me, once we exited the car in the ship hull and walked to our cabin, the only bump we had was avoided by my friends decision not to let us travel in the van with the driver Lenny's agent had sent to meet us at the ship.
"No! He has long hair. He looks like a musician. This is Italy. They will assume he has drugs and stop his car and search it. You will have a problem for sure."

It was hard to imagine the narrow mindedness of this; but God had provided someone with wisdom and I was willing to listen. So we got back inside of his Mercedes Benz with the van following us.

We drove smoothly through the police checkpoint at the port and exhaled. We did, in fact, look like a family.

In the rear view mirror we saw four Carabinieri approach the van as it was signaled aside. Within minutes, the driver exited the car. He was detained, and his van was searched, just as our friend said he would be. My mother and I gasped. We drove slowly away, unable to even express our gratitude to each other that we had chosen correctly.

We pulled into a gas station a few minutes down the road to wait for the driver of the van. He was a lovely young music tech, who never did drugs, was extremely kind and polite, and very grateful we weren't in the car with him.

As he helped us load our few bags into his van, I turned to say goodbye to my friend, who was crying. My heart dropped. I knew why. This was the beginning of a bigger goodbye. He had fallen in love with a girl who needed to experience life in the ocean and not in the fishbowl I had lived in, in Cagliari.

At the time, even after being saved and walking in communion with God through the nightmare that was my life for nearly two years, there was so much I didn't know about living for Jesus Christ. This man was one of the many casualties of the war against my actually learning about what surrender really meant. That would be the next leg of my spiritual journey; real true surrender.

For now, I was on a honeymoon with God and it seemed He still existed to bless whatever choices I made, even when they were wrong. My heart was often pure, while my actions lacked knowledge of Gods true desires and why. It's not that my friend was wrong, or that his intentions were not good toward my son and me. It's just that there was nothing right about them either. We both cried a deep painful cry. The kind of cry you cry when you know that a real goodbye is taking place. I could not, and would not, choose him over the gifts and miracles God was giving me to enable me to go home. I can never repay him for his kindness to us that day. I can never repay him for risking his own life and freedom to help me be free; but I could not repay him with the rest of my life. There was a calling out there that God had dispatched the armies of Heaven to secure for me and He would *not* lose the war for me yet.

As we drove away, still crying as I stared out the back window of the van at him, I watched him fade into the distance until I could no longer see his face flowing with tears. I stared into the distance and my thoughts turned again to the scripture, given me on that fateful night when I thought Miloj would kill me.

No temptation (trial) has overtaken you except what is common to mankind. And God is faithful; he will not let you be tempted (tested)

beyond what you can bear. But when you are tempted (tested), he will also provide a way out so that you can endure it.
1 Corinthians 10:13 (NIV)

I thought of the desperation and fear that had overtaken me. I thought of the hopelessness I had lived in, not even two years prior. Then I thought of all that God provided to enable me to endure my days here, not only in prison for three months, but for another year and a half of house arrest. In fact, I reflected, He had enabled me to endure in the most beautiful of ways with the most beautiful of people and events.

My tears fell, as the van rolled on. I thought of the dear friends who stood by my side, the ones I met and befriended in the residence; people like the man crying in a Mercedes behind us who risked his life for us.

I thought of Rosie and Nicoletta, who ran the residence reception, and the constant sisterhood we shared for nearly two years of holidays and conversations about life and our dreams as we grew up. I thought of their families, especially Rosie's. Her parents, Ninetto and Maria Cristina, had taken me in as if I was their daughter. They became Christian's godparents when I baptized him in the little church across the street from the residence. They were with me in the hospital room, holding my hand and coaching me, until they could do nothing but go to the chapel and pray me through the final hours of pushing Christian into the world.

I thought of Francesca and Toto and their beautiful little black curly haired boy, Alessandro, whom the lord used when I asked God if He would send me a rose, after three days of prayer, as a sign that He would take me home soon.

On the afternoon of my third day in prayer, as I sat alone reading my Bible in my room, a beautiful little boy, whom I saw for the first time in the residence the night before, while I was hanging out downstairs with Rosie and Nico, was standing at my door. I could hear his sweet voice as if it was yesterday.

"Ciao Cinzia, sono Allesandro. I brought you something." He held out a perfect red rose that was hidden behind his back, in his little 6-year-old hands. When the significance of what was happening hit me, I began sobbing so emotionally that I had to hug him and assure him that I was, in fact, happy.

I remembered walking down the hall with him to meet his parents for the first time. His mother, a beautiful raven haired woman, told me he had spoken of seeing a very nice lady the night before and he wanted to pick me a flower. I explained to her my little prayer pact with God and she began crying for she too was a woman of faith. I thought of her husband, Toto, one of the most effervescent characters I've ever known. He was larger than life and full of love for me. We spent hours on end talking about life, and about 'Beautiful,' the American soap opera Francesca was addicted to.

As the van rambled down the highway my tears turned to a smile as I could hear Toto's booming voice singing to me in the memories in my mind. 'Tu sei per me le donne piu bella del mondo." I was not the most beautiful girl in the world. His wife was. But, it sure made me laugh and smile and feel just a bit better about my growing frame. Italians celebrated pregnant women in a way we don't, and should, here.

I thought even of how, to dispel any possibility growing in me that my rose miracle could have been a coincidence, six months later, again on my third day of prayer, feeling sad and homesick, I asked God for another flower, any flower, as a sign that He would take me home to my family soon. I pondered even how I had apologized for needing a sign; knowing my faith should have been stronger by then.

The tears came again as I remembered how, on day three, someone knocked on my door. I wasn't expecting anyone so I called out, "Who is it?" In Italian.

"Ciao Cinzia, sono Ally." The sound of Alessandro's tiny little voice answered me.

"Alessando!!!!" I didn't know they were back! I swung the door wide open to swoop my little angel up in my arms and I found him standing there, yet again, this time with a huge smile and with a beautiful spring flower. I knelt down and cried. This time he hugged me knowingly and questioned, "Ancora Cinzia?"

"Si Ally, Ancora!" Again.

There was no end to the love He showed me. No end.

I contemplated Rosie and Nico's faces, as I hugged them goodbye just the afternoon before. I said I would see them the following week, after I returned from Milan, knowing I couldn't share any details with them, as I didn't want to risk involving them. I was aching inside at the thought that perhaps I would never see them again, while also filled with a joyful hope that they would one day see *me* in America.

The memories wouldn't stop flooding my mind and heart. I thought of nearly two years of people and kindnesses and provision. I never had need of anything. God surrounded me with love; tangible love that came from all kinds of people, young and old.

I remembered the actor who told me, one day when I was filled with questions, "Stay with the questions Cynthia." He knew that if I kept asking questions I would be given a lifetime of answers. God has always been revealed with great meaning, and purpose, in my questions.

I remembered, Louigi, the journalist who had a deep and abiding love for me and for Christian. I could always feel his compassion for me and his *need* to see me free; as if he understood that I was living a moment in time as a butterfly whose wings were clipped. I could see, that since he didn't share my faith, not knowing how long it would be before my wings were free, deeply saddened him.

I thought of the little old men who hung out in the bar off the lobby and the cacophony of dialects and accents that they had. Naples, Rome, Milan, Sicily; they made up a chorus of Italy's amazing regions and the nearly completely different languages that represented them.

I thought then of Suora Angela, as the Italian countryside whirred by. I remembered the countless trips to the doctor with me to see my funny, and extremely handsome gynecologist, who laughed a sigh of relief when I told him God told me to stop praying for a girl because I would be a better mom to a boy.
"Thank God." He said staring me straight in the eyes, always causing me to wonder how it was possible my obgyn looked like Sean Connery. "Because, young lady, for months I haven't known how to tell you that your daughter has a penis." He and I and Suora Angela laughed so hard we cried.

There were so many memories. How would I ever hold them all in my heart forever? How would I not forget what I didn't want to forget?

When I left the prison on my birthday, nearly two years prior, all the girls cried a mixture of happiness for me that I was leaving; and envy that they were not. They all said the same statement as I cried tears of joy while walking the stone corridors of Buoncammino Prison one last time.

"Mai guardare in dietro, Cinzia. Deve sempre guardare in diritto."

"Never look back or behind you Cynthia. Always look straight ahead."

The thing was that *my* straight-ahead would always include what was behind me. All that I am is affected by all that I was. Everything I know, until today, is because of everything that happened to me yesterday. In my heart I *never* wanted to blot out my time in an Italian prison and my pregnancy living under house arrest. This was the greatest period of my life that gave me the greatest gift of my life: my son and my faith.

Unbeknownst to me, as the van drove toward Milan and away from the port where Cagliari was now far in the distance, I would have years of fun and privilege and fame and friends in front of me. But, it was everything behind me that my heart would always go back to. It was everything behind me that I would never forget; the love that was shown me by so many as evidence of the love I had and have always had from my Father. I would never forget where I was saved; Where my life found its meaning and my calling was secured.

Not that there wouldn't be more struggles in the years to come, as I tackled Hollywood as a single mom, and dealt with relationships with worldly people, and not having enough fellowship to stand in. There would be more to learn and experience on my road to surrender. Especially, surrender enough to finally write this book feeling as if I have a smidgen of wisdom about why all our life messes are many times, our own fault and the fault of a major underlying culprit; our own emotional brokenness. There was more to come. So much more to come.

But on that day, back then, in the van driving toward Milan, where we would meet yet another friend, made in my time in Italy, who would step forward to help us; there was me and my mom and my baby and my God and my memories. I was so loved by Him. And I was going home.

32

HOME

So you handed them over to their enemies, who made them suffer. But in their time of trouble they cried to you, and you heard them from heaven. In your great mercy, you sent them liberators who rescued them from their enemies.
Nehemiah 9:27 (NLT)

After being saved, and returning home to California, I was in a bit of a haze as to what to do with my life. I prayed about it daily and I knew God would lead me. I simply vowed to keep my personal *wants* out of the equation. I actually had no more desire for fame, with the voracious appetite I had prior to spending nearly two years in Italy and getting saved in a prison, so praying and waiting was easy for me to do.

I had returned to California, after a three-day escape, that took me underground and into Switzerland, before arriving at Los Angeles International Airport, overflowing with emotions and tears as we pulled up to my sister's house. She had been terrified and worried, not knowing what happened, or where we were, because my mom and I went radio silent for three days after our distraught call home with news about my trial and the horrible, yet realistic, options pending my Supreme Court appeal.

Needless to say, when my sister, who was standing in her kitchen window doing dishes, saw our taxi pull up with me in it, I heard dishes drop; glasses break, and watched her scream before bursting into tears. My reunion, once home, was a celebration of laughter and tears from everyone; praise and worship from me. ·

Once home, I needed to remain in a place of stillness inside, because in those initial weeks fear drove everyone around me. My family was engulfed in discussing my life and what it should now be. I heard way to many discussions about how to hide me out to live on Lenny's island, in the Bahamas. I knew in my heart God didn't bring me home for all this. I retreated to prayer, asking Him to speak. He did.

I woke one morning from a dream in which I was told to go to a church called West Angeles Church of God in Christ. I had never been there before. I didn't even know if I knew anyone who had. As the day passed, an old girlfriend, an actress named Theresa Randle, called me and I explained my dream to her. She then told me her sister, Gwen, went to West Angeles.
"But, I'm supposed to go tonight?" I explained. It was Wednesday so I was confused about this part of my dream and its instructions.
"Gwen goes every Wednesday night for mid week service." Who knew? I smiled to myself. Our God is so far beyond us. We just need to sit and wait for His instructions to become clear, instead of question them.

Later that evening, I was told in my Spirit by an intensely strong leading, that I was to bring Christian with me and not leave him home with my mom. She felt that since I had never left him I didn't trust leaving him with her. That wasn't it. It was a leading from God. I explained to my mom, while Gwen listened. I felt that He had a message for me at this particular church, and I needed to go, and I had a sense that I was *supposed* to take Christian with me for some reason. She got it, as did Gwen. My mom had witnessed me hearing from God enough for nearly two years that she trusted the guidance I was receiving.

As the praise music in church started, Gwen realized I was carrying an arm full with Christian. He was squirmy and I kept getting distracted by needing to attend to him. She motioned for me to follow her to the back of the church and upstairs. When we got inside of a large room that had a wall of glass that looked inside the sanctuary I realized we were in a nursery.

"Oh no, it's ok. He can stay with me." I stated. It would be years before I became comfortable with him out of my eyesight. I may not be there fully, even now, and he's 25.

A woman approached us. She recognized my hesitation as she held her arms out. Christian was all too happy to jump into them.

"Don't worry. You can see us and we can see you. Look." I glanced out the large pane of glass, down into the sanctuary, and could indeed see where Gwen and I had left our bags. I then surveyed my child who was smiling and pulling at the woman's ear.

"OK. Thank you." He seemed fine so I relented.

The sermon began, and the sermon ended, and while I was moved, I didn't quite feel I had heard from God. There was something I hadn't received. I felt there was something more. I didn't know what to do so I was a little disappointed.

I followed Gwen through the crowd of people now leaving service. We walked back up the stairs, at the back of the church, to collect Christian. I stood patiently while other moms collected their kids from various women who were volunteers in the kids' room. After a few moments the woman holding Christian appeared with him laughing happily in her arms.

"Hi champ. I missed you so much. You have fun." I reached for him and she hesitated.

"Wait, I need to tell you something. God told me you came here tonight for a message from Him."

With that I stopped cold in my tracks. Gwen's eyes opened wide although she was not surprised. She too understood the supernatural and walked in faith in it.

"I have a gift. He speaks to me through children. He said you've just returned home from a very big and life changing experience."
Now, overflowing with emotions I opened my mouth to explain about Italy, and the last couple years, and what was going on, and everyone's fears that since my escape I needed to hide out in the Bahamas.

But nothing would come out of my mouth. I was literally trying to speak but no words were coming out. She just smiled at me, almost knowingly. "Its not for now. It's not for me to know now. One day you will tell everyone. But for now, He wants you to understand about your son. This child is very special. He's got a huge calling on his life. God told me that in his service in God's kingdom he will be exalted above many." She stared at me seriously, as if she wanted to be sure I understood the significance of what she was saying.

I'm not sure I did. I knew she was the one with the message God wanted me to hear, however. But did I understand, back then, the depth of what she was revealing to me about my son? I don't know. Back then I didn't even understand prophesy, and the gift of prophecy, which she clearly had. Through the years I've come to understand very clearly the significance of what she's saying because, now, I can state that I believe my son is a very significant voice to, and of, his generation. He also flows heavily in the gifts of the spirit; including prophecy.
"Raise him up to know Gods word. Take care of him. Good care." She said as she handed him back to me while I cried. I looked at Gwen standing at my side and she was crying also. The truth of what we just heard could not be escaped.

"He also said that what just happened to you is now behind you. There is no need to fear it. It's over. Go forward and live your life." My mouth was open. Tears poured from my eyes. Time stood still. There was only me, knowing that my Father was speaking. I was clear. I had come here tonight to hear from Him. He was not silent. The moment, powerful and affirming of so much, was overwhelming.

I stood there, holding Christian tightly, wondering how God could be so real yet doubted by people so much. He brought me home never to doubt again. He *never* brings you through to drop you off in doubt. Just hold on. He has a plan.

I will never forget God's words through her, to me, about Christian. Those words kept me going back to God for direction through the years when things came against him and me. Eventually, her prophetic insight caused me to lay on my face and beg God to take my career, my life, and whatever else he needed to, in order to save my son and get us walking boldly in His purposes for us. The revelation about my sons calling and purpose guided me in many ways over the years in understanding that, as a threat to the kingdom of darkness, I needed to be aware of attacks when they came against him. Those attacks came in the form of third grade teachers, basketball coaches at every level, and a few random kids and other people in authority, who were easily used by the enemy who wanted to eliminate a huge threat early on in life. I had experienced the same type of warfare against my calling from day one, so I was very aware of people in various disguises that were nothing more than Satan's tools against the journey God is taking my son on, for the benefit of his kingdom calling.

After service, it was her words that broke the confusion off my household when I returned home that night. I had heard from my Father. My decision was official. I announced to my mom, my sister, Lenny, and anyone who would listen, "It's over. I'm not living my life hiding out in The Bahamas or anywhere else. He didn't deliver me, for me to hide. I'm going forward with my life. Whatever that looks like. It's done. I'm free."

My mother voiced one thing adamantly, from the remnants of what she called good sense, which I recognized as her greatest fear.

"I certainly hope you don't think you can work on TV and call attention to yourself. At least live your life under the radar."

When I think of what she said then, I laugh all the time. Little did she know her words were deeply prophetic of everything I would never do.

Live under the radar. Ha!

33

F.A.M.E

"Then your fame went forth among the nations on account of your beauty, for it was perfect because of My splendor which I bestowed on you," declares the Lord GOD.
Ezekiel 16:14 (NASB)

I never doubted for a single moment that I would be famous. Not a real doubt. Not the kind of doubt that makes you give up or even deters you. I had been through so much that my attitude toward fame has always been, "Please I've been to prison. This is the good part." I could never become a completely entitled jerk as a famous person. How could I? I always had one foot, at least, grounded in a life changing experience, in which I learned humility and dependence on others. I have found it easy to remain humble and nice to people; unlike many famous people I've known.

My childhood had been fueled by my dreams of being a star. It was an escape route from my life, as many people use their careers as escape routes or identity providers. I wanted to live and work in Hollywood. I wanted famous friends, and red carpets, and private planes, and award shows, and glamorous dresses. I wanted to never be told no, to always be told yes, and to have any man I wanted as an accessory to my glamorous life; preferably famous ones and definitely the best looking ones. My little girl fantasy of fame was quite different than my heart toward it after getting saved.

Thankfully, I didn't get it when I wanted it.

There is a great lesson here in God's timing. We tend to always think we are ready for things...now. He knows when we are actually ready so that the things we want won't destroy us, limit us, define us, or pull us away from Him.

Oddly enough, TV just wasn't my goal any longer. I remember what I stated to Lenny's manager, Howard Kaufman, when he asked me why I didn't want to work on TV anymore. "Because Howard, I'm much to deep to be that shallow!"
He stared at me, chuckled, and replied, "Kid you're much to talented not to be a *little* shallow. You could give a whole lot more money to your church if you made a dime."

I had to laugh at the reality of that one; however, I was actually fairly content with the life I was living in my small apartment in Marina Del Rey back then. Even with no car, and little money, I loved the Marina. I could walk everywhere, including the beach. This is what I needed barely a year and a half past Italy, and less than six months past, God's revelation to me in church to get on with the business of living life.

I found this apartment when, after a year or so home, I knew it was time to leave my moms house and go be Christians mother instead of Linda's daughter. While I cannot say Linda was happy with the choices I made, in order to afford my own little apartment and life, she did respect me, eventually.
"Welfare?!" My mother shrieked.
"Yes, mom. I need monthly help and Christian needs health insurance and I need an apartment so we can have a home."
"You have a law degree from USC. Take the bar and practice law."
"Mom, after everything I've been through I know that I don't want to practice law. I want to write a book or something. I want to help people. I don't know. I just know that I have to hear from God about my life, and I have to make a life for Christian, and I can't do it sitting under you and being your baby. I have a baby myself now."

She eventually relented and accepted what she felt was a most embarrassing and shameful image; that of her eldest child, the golden one, about whom she bragged continuously, and the one whom she believed once had a very bright future, sitting in a welfare office asking for assistance. I remember thinking, quite confidently however, that I was the most blessed girl in the world because God provided a way for me to get an apartment; an apartment that should have cost so much more. Welfare or not I felt happy to be moving forward.

I found a cute place in a lovely building near the water, surprisingly. I loved that place. It had a waterfall in the garden outside my balcony so the sound of water always filled my place bringing in such peace. It was my incubator. When we moved in, after being at my mom's house for nearly a year, it was like being blessed with the most amazing gift. My time in Italy gave me a major appreciation for having my own place again.

Still unsure about what I would do in the long run, I eventually wrote a column for what a Christian startup newspaper, called LA Focus, that a dear friend's big sister started. She couldn't really pay me at first but I learned so much and loved the column that I wrote. It was called Through The Storm. I interviewed people and profiled how they got through difficult situations by relying on their faith.

I was honestly satisfied in so many ways, because of the spiritual place of strength and confidence I was in. The column was perfect for me to write. I loved our apartment and walking to the beach, and around the marina, with Christian in a stroller. I loved sitting in my room and reading my Bible to the sound of the waterfall. And, I loved watching Christian becoming a little toddler. He was such a joy. He was strong, assertive, and unbreakable in spirit like his mother. I often chuckled to myself about the strength I sensed inside him. He would be a force to handle.

I kept a journal through my time in Italy that I wasn't sure would become a book one day or not. I wrote daily for almost two years, knowing even then, that God would one day have me share my story. Our history is HisStory if we give it to Him. Eventually, Howard asked if I would let him read it. It was deeply personal and I was a bit hesitant, but I loved Howard, and I could tell he wanted to figure me out and help me in some way. I also wanted an opinion about what I wrote.

A week or so after sending him the book he called Lenny and chuckled saying simply, "I always thought she was just your cute sister. I never knew how brilliant she actually is, Lenny. She's a very deep young woman."

To which Lenny replied, "The deepest."

When Howard called me and raved about how amazing my talent as a writer was, I was extremely encouraged. Having gotten inside my dreams, and inside my head, after reading such personal memoirs, he prodded me about the childhood dreams I had of television and urged me to think about pursuing work on TV again.
"Cynthia, I watch you with people. I watch when you walk in a room. You have a natural ease and charm with people; all people. You need to be working on TV. It's not a dream that's unachievable." I didn't really know what to say.
"Thank you Howard. It just that..."
"Yeah, I know. You're to deep to be so shallow. But, you need to make a life for you and Christian and I think you can build a career in this, kid. Think about it. Pray about it. Whatever it is you do. Money doesn't have to be a bad thing." He was right. I smiled on the other end of the phone.
"You with me on Saturday?" He continued.
"Absolutely!" I replied. Howard and I did most Saturdays together at the racetrack. His wife, Sherry, hated going and I, having grown up loving watching the horse races with my grandpa, loved it. I loved our

Saturdays. Howard would pick me up, we would drop Christian off at my moms house, and he would slide me my two-hundred dollar betting allotment for the day with the agreement that we split our combined winnings.

Of course, being a single mom, I never bet my money. I always kept it. Howard would bet his first. Time always ran out before I could bet mine and so we would split his winnings happily. But he would always let me keep my original two hundred dollars. I loved hanging out with him and discussing my faith with him. He gave me great advice, as I considered working in TV again and navigating life as a single mom. I, in turn, provided a safe shoulder for him to cry on about Sherry, his beloved wife, who was battling ovarian cancer. They had experienced a number of rough years. And, I often prayed for him and her when we were together.

My little two hundred dollar race day gambling money, that I never gambled away, also meant I paid a bill, or sometimes, bought something Christian needed. Our Saturdays helped me so much as a single mom back then. I loved Howard tremendously for his heart toward me, and I always knew how deeply he loved me for the faith I sewed into him, at a time in life when I like to think he needed me, as much as I needed him. A lot of people tried to project a lot of things on the unending help and support he gave me in the initial years of launching my career, but I never cared at all what people thought. Sherry never seemed to care either. She and I loved each other and got along great. We knew that what Howard and I had was pure and beautiful. He was yet another blessing from God; a miracle provided to help me endure the times where life was more of a trial than it was easy.

I wish everyone in his life were intelligent enough to see the truth of our relationship and not be blinded by his or her own jealousies and insecurities. I have learned though, that life without real faith, and without a pursuit of Gods heart for others, leaves room only to project the twisted agendas of the flesh that you, yourself, might indulge in.

Life with faith, and with God's heart toward others, leaves room to see the many things God can achieve through how He uniquely made each of His kids. In God's design, it is in relationship with each other, that He accomplishes the many plans and purposes of His heart. When moving in the flesh, many people break the power of what God wants to do through relationships because they're small mindedness puts God in a box only as big as their mind can conceive. God doesn't exist in a box, however. He is infinitely bigger than our minds can conceive. We only hurt ourselves when we limit God. God is limitless.

To try and define the many unique and varied relationships I've had, especially with men, is a total waste of time. When God has been in them, and they've been Godly and not fleshly, I've seen purpose reveal itself for years. There is no limit to the amazing way men and women can nurture, love, encourage, and support each other if their initial fleshly desires or pursuits can be completely crucified and submitted to God's will.

34

MEN AND WOMEN VS. GODS PURPOSES

So God created man in his own image, in the image of God he created him; male and female he created them
Genesis 1:27 (NASB)

A few years past my humble welfare year and my early days with Howard, I became a successful TV personality in my own right.

I met many well-known and successful men in this season of life. Howard Kaufman, as well as my friend Teddy Forstmann, taught me incredible lessons about myself. To sum up, Howard taught me to believe in my ability and talent. Teddy taught me I was worth more than my ability and talent.

Between men and women, boys and girls, if God is kept first, flesh non-existent, you will see an array of God's purposes blossom. This is one more reason why purity is so important.

I became really close friends with Teddy, an older billionaire, with whom most people assumed there was a physical connection, I'm sure. I lived in his homes with Christian, drove his cars, and traveled for many years with him and his sons, Everest and Siya, as well as alone. We had an amazing and pure friendship, in which in our first week of knowing each other, I packed up my son and hopped on his plane with him to leave for Aspen and spend Christmas with him and his friends and two boys. We had an instant connection in the Spirit; that most wouldn't ever understand. At times we didn't understand it ourselves. But whatever *it* was it lasted till the day he died.

By day six of meeting him, nestled into a beautiful room for Christian and I in his Aspen home, we woke up on a Sunday before Christmas and went to church together. He watched me intently from the corner of his eyes through most of service in the beautiful Catholic Church we attended together in Aspen. I prayed for him, as my new friend, and for God's purposes to always be done in our relationship.

When we left church and were at home later that day Teddy and I sat talking in the living room. He seemed melancholy. He had just gone through a breakup with a long-term rather toxic girlfriend. I was also going through a breakup with someone I met on my first job on Television at VH1.

Teddy's world, which was now my world, consisted of agenda driven love and anticipated gain from friendship. I had none of this in me. "You've completely restored my faith in women." He said sincerely. "You really are the last good girl in the world."
"No." I stated with a sly smile. "I'm just the last good girl in *your* world." With that he tossed a handful of peanuts at me from the silver bowl in the living room and we both laughed heartily. We laughed a lot together through the years to come actually.

Teddy and I met at a dinner given for me, and for the gorgeous Faith Hill, by a large magazine that I was featured in. She was the cover story. We had an immediate combustion of laughter and bonding that night, seated at dinner next to each other. So much so, that we met for lunch the next day and talked for hours. He told me he was leaving on his plane for Aspen the following day, after breakfast, for the Christmas holidays.

"What are you doing for Christmas?"
"No plans really." I was in the final stages of my breakup with my current boyfriend of four years.
"Come to breakfast and bring your son and come to Aspen with me."

"Uhhh, excuse me?"

"No, no, nothing inappropriate. There will be a group of us. Five of my oldest friends. You'll have your own room. It's a great time." I trusted him from day one. He was a good man. In business he was a brilliant, innovative, man who pioneered many things including the private jet and Gulfstream. As a friend to me he was supportive, encouraging, and taught me so much, as did Howard, Lenny, Robbie, and the handful of amazing men friends God blessed me with. He was an example to me of how God wanted me to be treated as His daughter. There were private planes and great adventures and lots of money with Teddy. However, It was the respect, the expectation of high moral character, and the encouragement to become much more than I often saw that I should be, that changed my life.

"I've never been good at relationships but I'm not bad at friendship." He said as we both laughed at the peanuts all over me.
"I suck at relationships but all my friends are men. I'm great at friendships with guys. So, this is gonna work out great." I smiled.

I remember walking over and plopping down in his lap and he stated, "Wait, does this mean there are no fringe benefits? I can't touch you?! I think I'm in love with you and it happened in ten minutes."
"No, you're not. We've known each other five days." I laughed. I was extremely drawn to him, but we both knew we were likely both to damaged to navigate a relationship without ruining it. God had much bigger purposes than what we may have otherwise explored.
"Maybe I am." He was smiling. I loved his smile. It was full of everything he had a hard time saying.
"We don't need to define anything Ted. Let's just...be. God's got some plan in it that He will reveal in time I'm sure."

That night at dinner, with friends, he nicknamed me, "The Countess Mustn't Touch It.' This would stick till the day he passed away. My nickname, Countess, was our little reminder that if we didn't touch what God had given us we would be friends till we died. This bond was sealed in church that first weekend. He had seen my love for Jesus and I saw his heart to find the same self-love that I had often struggled to find.

Time would introduce me to the fact that my close friend was an icon in business and philanthropy. I met an array of interesting people through him. From people like, Nelson Mandela and Henry Kissinger to people like James Taylor and Hugh Grant. He introduced me to Oprah Winfrey one night, at his 60th birthday event, in the backyard of his Beverly Hills estate. Christian and I would eventually live in that beautiful home for some time while I transitioned into my new job hosting my own NBC late night show 'Later w/Cynthia Garrett.' The show made me the first African American woman to ever host a *network* late night show.

"Oprah, this is my dear friend, the Countess." Give her some good advice. She just got her own show. She shook my hand curiously, and dismissively, and replied, "Countess of what?"

Teddy answered matter of factly, "The Countess Mustn't Touch It." He then walked away chuckling, leaving me standing there.

"It's a nickname." I stated. I'm sure she projected all kinds of stuff into that moment. Teddy loved it. He loved to challenge people and to put them on the spot with all their preconceived notions. I was always able to handle him because I usually don't have any pre-conceived notions about anyone or anything. God has taught me to take everyone at their word unless He makes something different very clear to me. Others have a hard time with this, but as scripture says; love thinks the best!

God blessed me, through my men friends, to learn many valuable lessons of identity that were rooted in my need to be taught self-esteem. I see so many young women in the world today who don't have a clue how to value themselves. Sadly, it takes many women time to even understand when a man is valuing them. Yet, we need men to be men of God so badly. It's like the chicken and the egg so I don't know where the problem began first. However, I know we as women, control the bar because we possess what men need and desire. If we set the rules around this game where God wants them set, men would have no choice but to seek God for how to win our hearts, minds, and our bodies, in marriage.

Instead, we accept a lowered bar and in turn we've ended up not understanding what it means to be valued or to value ourselves. Our fears of being alone, and never getting the guy we want, have caused us to use our sexuality to win men's attention, and to expect that they expect us too. In turn, if men saw their value, they wouldn't so quickly hop into a woman's bed, understanding the power they have to destroy not just themselves, but the women, and any kids that may come from the union.

As a reminder of this lesson I still wear Teddy's favorite Jaeger Le Coultre watch that he bought for me for my birthday the year I got my first big network show, on NBC.

He presented me with a box over breakfast at the Peninsula Hotel in Beverly Hills. I opened the box and was struck by the beautiful Reverso that flips from a day option to a diamond encrusted evening option. He wore one similar to it. I looked at him stunned, and then I became awkward and started crying. In my mind, I assumed that a gift that cost this much meant that he was now expecting to have sex with me. After about a year and a half of close friendship, I was then living in his Beverly Hills estate with Christian. I felt free from the breakup I went through in NYC, had an amazing new show, and was being given a new beginning. But, I was floored by his gift and confused by pressure as to what it meant.

To which he replied, "Countess, for Gods sake, your generation is so screwed up! Can't a man give you something expensive because *you're* priceless? That watch is worth far less to me than you are. It's a gift. There are no expectations to sleep with you. Who did this to you? You can't conquer the world if you're always late. I figure a watch is a great gift because I love you."

He, like Howard, sewed so much more self-esteem into me than either of them would likely ever realize. I sat there in a flurry of emotions; happiness, sadness about the reality of what he said, and revelation into an issue deep inside that still lay there dormant. I truly didn't understand much about my value to God or men.

I tell my son all the time, to always be God's guy with his girl friends because they need to see and experience a Godly man more than he could ever know. Women's self esteem is so broken in the world today. My whole journey home to my identity has been all about coming to terms with who I am and how valuable I am to God. He never expects anything in return. He desires our love, but we don't have to give much more than that, in all honesty. His grace is so sufficient. He doesn't need TV shows about Him, and churches, and books, and works. He just desires our love relationship with Him. We don't have to work at loving Him. It's so easy when we understand how much we are loved and valued. In the same way, we don't have to work at being loved by the right man. He will just love and value you for who you are; free of work, pretense, or perfection.

Men like this, who've been examples of God's love to me, have marked my life forever. I only wish Ted had loved himself as much as he desired for me to love myself. He used to always say to me, when discussing yet another girl he was dating, while always very clear about her agenda, "Countess, the one constant in all these equations is me. I am broken."

I so wish I knew then, what I know now, about the inner healing of emotional brokenness. Even so, God had much bigger purposes for my friendship with Theodore J. Forstmann. Not allowing our brokenness to ever dominate our initial rooting in Christ, in that church in Aspen, preserved Gods ultimate purposes.

As time passed, I too would sometimes become confused about what God was doing or actually intended for my friendship with him. But clarity came after twelve years of dinners, and trips, and vacations, and tears, and relationship.
"Countess, I have cancer in my brain and I need to tell you before its all over the press." I nearly suffocated on my own breath.
"What, Ted? What does this mean?"
"It means I'm gonna fight like hell. But...its the same one Ted Kennedy had." I could hear where he believed this was going. I heard fear and resolve, mixed in with a rather shaky belief, in whether or not he could beat it. There was so much emotion in this one moment that we both felt on opposite ends of the phone. Then it all became clear. All of a sudden, I knew why I had the favor with him that I had enjoyed for nearly thirteen years.

I knew *why* God had given me years on his helicopters and private planes and years in his homes at his side. I knew *why* I was allowed the access and privilege to him that many would kill for. It was never about me. Even though it was also about me. It was why God kept us from going to the obvious place our attraction and love might have taken us. After that first day in church, the first week we were blessed with each other, we had promised each other to keep God first. That was what he had always seen and loved in me and it's what I always saw and loved in him: God. Something nobody else would ever think about him or about me back then. This is why he needed me. After years of my own inner searching and growing I realized I would now be his lifeline to the truth. As with Esther, I was there for such a time as *this*.

"Teddy, you know I love you right?"

"I know you do Countess."

"Then hear me out. Have you ever really given your life to Jesus? Not just go to church, but I mean a real relationship before every other one?"

He began to cry. They were tears born of Satan's lie that we are too sinful and unworthy of being saved, after years of messes and mistakes and living for oneself. "Countess, I'm not perfect. I've lived a fairly flawed life. I mean I've tried but man I'm not..." He trailed off. The guilt of his sin, and the recognition that no matter what the world saw of his many achievements and accomplishments, he himself felt like a flawed, bad, man, burdened him.

"I've lived far short of the glory of God, Countess. Far short."

"Teddy we all need a Savior, my love. *Nobody* is perfect. Yet, while we were still sinners Jesus Christ died for our sins. The Bible says that. While we were still sinners He died for us. Our messes do not shock Him. Funny, now I know *why* I'm in your life."

"What do you mean, Countess?" He asked quietly.

"Ted, let me lead you to Christ. Just say the sinners prayer and repent and get right."

"Pray. I don't even know if I know how, Countess. I haven't prayed in a long time."

"All ya gotta do is repeat after me. I will show you. Do you want that?"

"Yes, I do."

And with that Theodore J. Forstmann, aka Teddy Bear, aka Ted, aka my Teddy, gave his life to Christ. I cried. He cried. Purpose, where he and I were concerned, had finally revealed itself that day, on my telephone. I would later pray with his two sons, Everest and Siya, and make surprise trips popping in on him at one of his homes, to feed him or just to sit with him and love him. Everyone around him, who I thought was so close to him, seemed so unable to show him the kind of love he needed in those last years. People he cared for financially, for many years, didn't show up for him in the way I believe they should've emotionally. Even a woman he was seeing, that all of his closest friends, and he himself, found to be a supreme joke, was admittedly about the facade of his life and not the part that was real. Inside him, in many ways, he was dying and had died years prior for lack of love. Real love. But God didn't leave him alone. God showed up. No matter what messes we make of our lives He continuously shows up presenting us with one important option; the option to choose Him.

I had tremendous peace in the remaining years with him. From the day he chose to ask Jesus to be His Savior for real, I knew he would be ok. I also knew my work was done, which made me decide to pass on going to his funeral. I had experienced a dying of the flesh and a resurrection of life with my friend, Teddy. There was nothing more significant to celebrate or experience. And, I had no desire to mourn. I still do not mourn him. I miss him tremendously. There are times I want to call him, or laugh about something I've read with him, or share something I'm feeling with him. But, I know where he is and I know I will see him again.

And, most importantly, he knows that I know. This excited him too. Nothing made him prouder than to know that I had found my way to an even deeper place of relationship with God than when we met. He loved the fruit of my complete surrender by this point in time to God as Lord of my life. He loved how my brain started working and how my mind was beginning to see more sides of an issue than just the one the world presented. He loved the change of values and morals he saw me embrace.

Intensely possessive of me, and never interested in me being in a relationship with anyone except him, he never liked any guy I ever mentioned the possibility of bringing around to meet him. But, he had met Roger and he was happy that I was engaged to a good man. He was proud that I chose celibacy until my marriage night. He knew the value I had finally found in, and for, myself. And, he was so proud that

I was stepping boldly into my identity like never before in these choices.

It all had such purpose when I think about it. It was Rogers arrival in my life, which collided with my voracious desire for knowledge, that gave me the clarity and the boldness from which God was able to use me to finally speak into Teddy's life. Something I could boldly do because we weren't damaged and compromised by ever having become physical with him. Some of his last words to me were, "Countess, thank God you've got so much inside you to say that's important. I hated all that crap talk about Hollywood and famous people. They're all so...boring and unimportant. It's just to stupid to talk about."
I remember looking at him as we laughed and all I could say was, "Ha! You hypocrite." He was never one to mince words.

35

SUCCESS NOW WHAT

I know your deeds, that you are neither cold nor hot; I wish that you were cold or hot. So because you are lukewarm, and neither hot nor cold, I will spit you out of My mouth. 'Because you say, "I am rich, and have become wealthy, and have need of nothing," and you do not know that you are wretched and miserable and poor and blind and naked, I advise you to buy from Me gold refined by fire so that you may become rich, and white garments so that you may clothe yourself, and that the shame of your nakedness will not be revealed; and eye salve to anoint your eyes so that you may see. 'Those whom I love, I reprove and discipline; therefore be zealous and repent. 'Behold, I stand at the door and knock; if anyone hears My voice and opens the door, I will come in to him and will dine with him, and he with Me. 'He who overcomes, I will grant to him to sit down with Me on My throne, as I also overcame and sat down with My Father on His throne. 'He who has an ear, let him hear what the Spirit says to the churches.'"
Revelation 3:15-22 (NASB)

If Ted was a barometer throughout my career, Howard Kaufman was the fire starter. Through Howard, God reignited my passion for my dreams, and launched my career. He encouraged me and prodded me and re-connected me with the fact that I had actual talent and not just childhood fantasies that were grounded in nothing. By causing me to look at my dreams again, and to look at the good I could achieve from having a podium to speak from, Howard awakened my awareness in the fact that these dreams were not entirely my own stupid fleshly fantasy, but perhaps God's will for my life.

Not long after those Saturday trips to the racetrack started, Howard took over financial support of me, I got off welfare, and he tough loved me into hosting, producing, directing, and editing, my first one hour late night variety and interview show, which he financed. The more I prayed, the more driven I became, and the more I realized that I had not in fact gotten over my dreams, I had simply surrendered them to God in Italy. This was good.

When our dreams, desires, and relationships are submitted and surrendered to Him we can have them and not be controlled by them. When our dreams, desires, and relationships, are surrendered to God we realize that they are not for our benefit, but for use by God for whatever benefits He chooses. Yes we benefit from being blessed to do what we may have always dreamed of but our first thoughts should be about how God wants His kingdom to benefit. Though He calls us friends, we are still His servants.

This is a potent thing to understand and submit to, on a deep level, when fame is an integral part of what occurs if you achieve your dream. I did not want to lose myself and my faith in fame. I did not want to lose God in the busyness of success. I loved Him so much and I had been through so much to find the place of peace I had found inside with God, that I never would have thought my relationship with Him could be jeopardized.

But, in all honesty, as I ascended the ladder of success, and collected one famous friend and important person after the next, I was fairly ill equipped to retain a solid foundation in Christ. There was still so much that I needed to find out about God, and His heart, toward the way we live and love. And, my identity was still unclear because I still had a tremendous amount of brokenness responsible for many mindsets that affected my life. My relationship with my Savior, who had moved mountains for me, and would move them yet again, would most certainly be jeopardized by my success.

I did not understand the issue of pre-marital sex, amongst other things, with any real depth or commitment and this was a big one for me. I was single and I still had big trust and intimacy issues with men that hindered my ability to discover my real identity. I was long past having an extremely casual attitude about sex for sure. I knew now, at least, that it was important. I just thought, like nearly every Christian I meet, that it was OK if you felt you were in love.

This is just the beginning. There were so many things, big and small, that I didn't have God's perspective about as I went through the busy years of my secular career. I did not think cursing was wrong. It was just the language of the day. I did not understand that much of my TV diet was polluted with demonic agenda. It was just what there was to watch on TV. I was saved. Yes. But, I didn't understand what it meant to walk out my faith in a real world that walked the opposite way of it. I didn't understand what it meant to be a Christian; the Charles Finney kind of Christian that I aspire to be today.

Don't copy the behavior and customs of this world, but let God transform you into a new person by changing the way you think. Then you will learn to know God's will for you, which is good and pleasing and perfect.
Romans 12:2 (NLT)

The bar for my faith today, was recently raised by something my brother, Philip Mantofa, said. Philip and his wife, Irene Saphira-Mantofa, have the largest church in Southeast Asia. Based in Indonesia, Philip's church is beyond an example of what a church should be. Not because of its 45,000 members, but because of their heart for Jesus. Certainly because of the heart of their leader. Philip made a statement that has elevated my mind to question my heart yet again. He said, " If Jesus is not worth dying for He is not worth living for." This statement is from a man with a price on his head and a very high ranking on Isis hit lists.

Back then, however, while I navigated the early years of walking red carpets and experiencing worldly success, I thought the bar for my faith was high, simply because I believed and had encountered God in miraculous ways in Italy. I thought this assured a level of closeness and depth that I didn't quite realize I still had to work at to grow, earn, or deserve.

However, I was a baby Christian, headed toward Hollywood, with zero friends who were living for Jesus. Faith first was not a concept I really understood. Like many Christians today, Jesus was amazing, yes. He blessed my choices, gave me peace in my trials, and seemingly answered many of my prayers so I must have been fine in whatever condition I was in. I was, after all, much more than a Sunday Christian while living in my Marina Del Rey apartment years ago. However, I lacked enough solid foundation, inner healing, and clear purpose to know that I was walking back into a danger zone. It was a different type of danger zone than the one I had lived in, and lived through, prior to Italy; but a danger zone nonetheless.

My fire, without other flames around to keep the fires burning, became the lukewarm fire that Revelation speaks of, that no Christian wants to admit to. The kind in jeopardy of being spit out for neither being hot nor cold. I went to mid week Bible study, for a few years after I was saved, and watched TBN catching a good word here and there, and even read my Bible; albeit less and less as the months turned into years in Hollywood. My close friends, while all Christians, we're just like me. Eventually, chasing Jesus turned into chasing careers first, chasing money second, then chasing Jesus last, if even chasing Him at all, on most days. An understanding of brokenness still years away, I'm not surprised that the chaos of having a career, and the deception of being 'good spiritually,' because gods blessings continued to pour out, left me blind to the fact that I was once again going in the opposite direction of the life I was called to.

Oh how the mighty can fall. When I tell the story of my life prior to being saved, and everything I went through in being saved, and all the miracles God performed for me, I'm virtually astonished that I got so swept up in being famous, and chasing my career, that the God who gave me the career, in the first place, became someone I checked in with occasionally. I always professed my undying love to Him and for Him to others. I was always quite bold and vocal about being a Christian even when it wasn't PC. In my heart, nobody would ever get me to deny Jesus. Period. However, since I was chasing the only career I knew to chase, in the only way I knew how to chase it, I eventually looked like the world, dressed like the world, walked like the world, and talked like the world.

I didn't realize that perhaps the reason I was allowed to be bold and vocal about my faith in Hollywood is because it lacked any real power or sanctification from the world. I was neutralized by sin I didn't realize had crept back into my life, as I rose in the ranks of the Hollywood in-crowd.

As long as others around me felt un-judged or un-challenged by my faith things were easy. I never experienced persecution for being a believer at all. As long as sin and compromise were fine with me nobody cared if I called myself a Christian. Why would they? I certainly wasn't shining any light of truth in my behavior so that others felt awkward or confronted in their darkness.

I mastered the part about loving everyone. It's the part about not living like everybody else that I failed at. Since I was chasing the only career I knew to chase, which existed only in the world, I eventually looked like the world, dressed like the world, walked like the world, and talked like the world.

That's how it is, not just with fame, but also with any career that brings respect and money and privilege and access to the things of the world. Materialism can so easily replace spiritualism. Before you know it you look up and realize you've been so busy shopping, and traveling, and enjoying the fruits of your hard labor, and God's blessings, that you forgot where you placed your relationship with God. You check in, but not deeply, or for any length of time. You acknowledge Him with your words, of course, but your actions acknowledge a desire to serve your own flesh more than Him. You realize that your kid, or kids, are lost and have no clue about a personal relationship with Jesus. And, worse, you realize that you, yourself, have been the worst witness imaginable to your own child of what it means to live for Christ.

All of a sudden, the great things you wanted to do with all your money and power for the Kingdom, and for others, you're doing for yourself. Then when there isn't enough money anymore, you can't do for the Kingdom or for others, because if you're honest you'll admit that you used it all for your own selfish gain and pleasure.

The truth stings doesn't it?

But, this is where I ended up. This is where you will likely end up if you continue on, blinded by your own ways. I say this as a strong admonishment to the body of Christ, especially in America, today. Wake up. There are more of you sleep walking through His grace than there are those who persecute the church around the entire globe.

But ye are a chosen generation, a royal priesthood, a holy nation, a peculiar people; that ye should shew forth the praises of him who hath called you out of darkness into his marvelous light:
1 Peter 2:9 (KJV)

After years of living exactly the childhood fantasy I had dreamed of I found myself depleted, empty, aware that God was not only missing from my career He was missing from His throne in my life. I had become stagnant. I believed, but I had stopped growing spiritually. I was not a 'peculiar' person, in that I was so filled with Him and the knowledge that I was part of a holy nation, that I lived differently and with the responsibility I'm called to toward God's purposes and others. Instead, I was not peculiar at all. I was one of the world's in-crowd, dying, while separated from the vine spiritually.

My career, however, flourished while my spiritual life suffocated. Howard accompanied me into VH1 and between the power piece in the music world that he was, and the fact that I was Lenny Kravitz's sister, I was given a shot on air within a month of signing to a huge agency with an important agent, named Mark Itkin. The icing on the cake was when the channel, and everyone else, realized I was incredible on air. I lied about having ever even seen a TelePrompter before, and sat down and worked off of one as if I had been doing it for thirty years. I knew I was good. I knew I had a natural ability. And, it was all easy to me, because I had been to hell and back so everything was easy to me. Ha!

I was given live shows to do without a prompter and we discovered that I was even better. My education, travel, and exposure, provided a backdrop with my own wisdom, gained through life experiences to speak to anybody. I was offered show after show, and deal after deal. I was given a huge NBC late night show within a few years of walking into Mark, my agent's office, saying I wanted to be the first black woman a network hired and gave a late night show too. In a white, comedian, male dominated, world I wanted a shot. I wanted a show I could ask intelligent questions on. That came in the form of Later w/Cynthia Garrett.

Things came, things ended, and I moved on to the next show, the next channel, the next network, until eventually I conquered my desire to write by penning four screenplays and selling a half hour series to ABC network. I became the first celebrity columnist at In Style Magazine and wrote for other life style magazines along the way including my favorite; LA Confidential. I traveled the world, stayed only in suites, and flew privately more than commercially. My friends were not just the normally wealthy, but the abnormally wealthy, like Teddy. My life was blessed beyond belief. My childhood dreams were likely not even as good as my reality became in many ways. Not even my dreams for my love life were as incredible. I had a line of men in love with me. They were famous, rich, powerful, sexy, successful men. They were smart. They were leaders. They were everything a woman would want; except surrendered to Jesus.

I achieved so much that I took, for granted. One miracle after the next lined up to start my career in unprecedented ways. I literally began at the top in every way. In hindsight, I am so grateful. My only remorse is that I was to spiritually immature to understand the significance of what was handed to me, because I had stopped growing spiritually, and stagnated at about three years old.

Yet, I was mature enough, after years of feeling a growing call inside me to go deeper still, that I looked around me and realized there was a void. It existed inside everyone I knew. It existed inside myself. Something was missing and no matter how much we all had, there would always be the threat of depression and unhappiness because of the one missing component; a deep and dependent relationship with a living God. Somewhere in all the excess I realized that many of the people I knew, and loved, had nowhere to go apart from their things or the people they knew. But I did. I knew where to go. I knew that it was time once again to go there. I knew that the prophecy spoken over my son was haunting me because I had dropped the ball and, now fourteen and plagued by Hollywood identity confusion, I needed him to know God immediately. I knew that my friends, and the people I loved and love, all needed me to go there. Because *there* was where the answers were. *There* is where the answers are. I realized that I had been saved time after time because I was called to be a bridge between the kingdom and the world and while I enjoyed tremendous comfort in the world I was in it but not of it.

My Father wanted me to be a witness to those around me that He wanted to touch and to reach and to love. I had gotten selfish with what I was given and made my career about me and my purposes instead of about God and His. Sadly, this is the state of vanity the world lives in today.

I forgot I was His servant because I was so busy being His friend.

And what do you benefit if you gain the whole world but lose your own soul? Is anything worth more than your soul?
Matthew 16:26 (NLT)

Nothing is worth more than your soul.

36

SURRENDER

God paid a high price for you, so don't be enslaved by the world.
1 Corinthians 7:23 (NLT)

Once I became 'successful' my greatest idol was myself. Dying Star, by Jason Upton, expresses such a deep condition of fame and success that I am certain anyone who really listens to it would be convicted to repentance. For me, a time to get on the threshing floor eventually came.

You've got your best man on the front side
You always show your best side
And evil's always on the other side
You say this is your strategy
But son I hope you take it from me
You look just like your enemy
You're full of pride
We better trash our idols if we want to be
In the army of the Lord
And the greatest idol is you and me,
We better get on the threshing floor
When will we learn that God's strategy
Is giving glory to the Lord?
We better trash our idols if we want to be
In the army of the Lord
Star how beautiful you shine
You shine more beautiful than mine
You shine from sea to shining sea
World-wide is your strategy
But shinning star I hope you see
If the whole wide world is staring straight at you
They can't see me.

It is the last line of this song that described my entire successful existence. I had worked very hard for all eyeballs to be on me. I was comfortable with people's stares. I reveled in their stares, and eventually I felt I deserved their stares. But when I was hit with the reality that the lyrics to this song so perfectly explained, I knew that I was full of pride. The whole wide world was staring straight at me and they could in fact no longer see Him. When confronted with the fact that I knew deep in my heart, in a very profound way, that I was bought with a very high price there was only one thing I could do.

After years of private planes, and billionaire boyfriends, and the most famous movie star lovers, I got on my face and cried. I prayed a deep, desperate, prayer. A prayer as important, perhaps, as any prayer I prayed in Italy. It was a prayer of surrender.

"God take it all. Take everything; the house, the car, the career, the friends. I don't care. Just get me back to you. Get my life to become the life you want it to be. I know you saved me for more than this. So what is it? I surrender. I surrender it all right now, and if I never spend another day on TV, or as someone others know, I don't care. Please help me find my real identity; the one you created for me before the world told me what I was and how I was to be. We've been through too much together Father. Help me, and help my son, who's beginning to get lost in the world I thought I was right to raise him in. You told me that in his service in your kingdom he would be exalted above many. Father he doesn't know anything about your kingdom. I didn't raise him as you told me. I failed you and him. Please save him, let him know you. I have been so blessed by you but I have forgotten you in the blessings. I'm sorry Father. I surrender it all right now."

In Jesus name I prayed. In Jesus name I begged. In Jesus name I cried.

I had secretly dreamed for many years working in secular TV that I could be like Joyce Meyer and change women's lives. Nobody in my world knew who she was, but I did. Even though my relationship with God was left in the back of a limo while I went inside to the party, I always had at least one TV in my house on TBN; the channel introduced to me by River's parents years before.

I knew that my fame and my job meant nothing compared to what a woman with my fame and my job preaching the gospel looked like. If I wasn't going to be a woman who changed the world why bother I thought! What were the fame and the privilege and all the open doors about anyway?

Who cared about relationships with billionaire men, if at the end, like with Teddy, the love we shared didn't lead them to the cross to get saved. Who cared if I was host of a big network show, or starred in a movie, or sold a TV series, if God wasn't glorified in some way that truly changed the lives of the lost and hurting?

There had to be more I thought as I cried out to Him. There had to be more. I knew the calling on my son's life was huge yet he didn't even know the One he was called to. I had dropped the ball and not raised him rooted in the Word; because I wasn't really rooted in it anymore. He went to the best, private, secular schools in California. Money couldn't buy better. But, they had driven God so far outta those schools, long before I enrolled my son, that all I did was confuse his identity, and make it harder for him to believe in God at all; much less Jesus Christ his risen Savior.

But, I wouldn't accept defeat at this juncture. My God was too big. I knew what He was capable of. So, I surrendered my life, and my son's life to Him. I didn't care what it took, or where He took us. I'm ready Jesus was all I could think.

37

THE COST OF SURRENDER

Then he said to the crowd, "If any of you wants to be my follower, you must turn from your selfish ways, take up your cross daily, and follow me.
Luke 9:23 (NLT)

I think the least understood concept in Christianity today is surrender. Repentance is understood. Being saved is understood. Surrender is a mystery. What does it mean to surrender? Whatever it means one thing is clear; walking with the Lord in the fullest measure of your calling is impossible without it. There will always be too much that you don't understand, like, or feel to resist and walk away from. Without surrender you will always follow your feelings in those times. When you're surrendered to God you will not walk away, you will not resist, and you will continue even when you don't understand, simply because as a surrendered vessel one often understands that God's will can be radically different than your own.

I have come to learn that surrender is a complete letting go of your own will. It's a total acceptance of whatever God wants, wills, and desires. In an understanding of God's word, one hopes that the many things one faces in surrendering can be understood and walked out. Many times, however, they're not understood. As in the situation I faced next which, while terrified, tested my ability to surrender to God's will, against my desire to watch my son grow up, see him marry, hold my grandchildren and live life truly walking in the destiny I always knew God had for me, but had not yet experienced.

I was diagnosed with cancer. It seemed surreal; after all I had gone through to finally find the faith and the courage to walk away from everything in my life that I felt impeded my spiritual journey, only to be confronted with not having the chance to make that journey at all. Part of me felt certain this was a spiritual attack that I would overcome, the other part of me was deeply scared, and another part of me felt nothing at all except the need to walk through the challenge, day by day.

Roger had entered our life, within months of my prayer of surrender, and the following two years together had been a great adventure with him; not that it was an easy adventure at all. From meeting each other on the plane and discovering that we were going to marry there was much to navigate with Christian and with my deeper dive into my relationship with Christ. There were constantly challenges and questions to be confronted.

On top of our own challenges to become a couple, we were struggling to help Christian, find a comfort zone with Roger. My then moody, angry, scared, pre-teen son, resisted him entirely. The fact that he did resist him, without any clear explanation admittedly, let me know it was not his resistance, but the enemy who did not want me to walk any further into the clarity that was coming into my life because of Roger's spiritual knowledge; which I was soaking up like a sponge.

I understood that my surrender had brought on a lot of spiritual resistance to what was happening in my life in the natural realm. I called out to God giving him control of everything in my life. I knew that I had heard from God about Roger and followed His voice to prepare to marry him. I was devouring the word again. I was armed with deeper questions and receiving deeper revelations than I ever had before. As I understand spiritual warfare; Satan was scared. The armies of God in my life were advancing. The enemy's response to all this was round after round of spiritual attack.

The next attack, since career confusion by doping me into a pleasure filled stupor with success didn't work, was hard, heavy, and scary. I almost lost my mother: the undisputed heavyweight champion of my family. God was faithful, and in this attack he allowed me to see my future husband's commitment to, not just me, but also my family. For over a month, Roger stood with my sister and I as we handled my mother's life, bills, doctors, and medical decisions. He was a rock in keeping us standing on The Rock. He came through in ways only a husband would; covering us in prayer and handling the chaos of my mother's checkbook when we needed.

For a year after her illness, life returned to normal, and Roger and I were back to trying to give Christian the love and support he needed to envision life with a man who loved us in a way, and with a consistency, that he had never really experienced before. Time and prayers and inner healing would win him over in years to come.

With my mom out of the hospital and on her feet, I suppose the enemy of my soul was terrified that I had regrouped, so he came after me with an attack like none I had ever experienced.

I had always felt invincible; fearless actually. I was certainly never one to be fearful of illness. Yet, I couldn't shake three months of feeling like something was physically wrong with me. For three months, I went to every doctor imaginable in search of why my stomach looked and felt three months pregnant with bloat. I experienced constant pain, irritation, and discomfort. I was miserable and I knew something was wrong. The Holy Spirit drove me with urgency and a certainty that there was something *off* with my body. I just knew it.

I thank God for the relentless push He kept me in to figure out what the problem was. I recognize this as one of the miracles of provision that would be easy to overlook in the natural if I wasn't so aware in my spirit that there was something supernatural always driving my knowledge and my Spirit. God knew and He was literally making me know. I believe that surrender operates most effectively in this way. When you're surrendered you listen and hear from the Holy Spirit deep inside and you act on what He is telling you; even if five doctors find you irrational.

After three months of no diagnosis and worse, misdiagnosis, in the natural, we finally found the oversight by the gastroenterologist that would have taken my life, absent God's leading, and a desperate call I made to my gynecologist, a long time friend. He offered to review every single test that had been performed the past three months with Roger and me. In reading through tests and exams we finally found a comment by a radiologist that alluded to a mass found in my stomach lining that might require 'further clinical management.'

In less than ten days I was on an operating table. It turned out I had tumors in my stomach lining. It was cancer. The question looming heavily in my surgeon's mind was what kind of tumors and how bad were they.

Roger stayed by my side and read the word to me every day for a month. The fact that he never left my side was one thing, but the way he never left my side was what was impressive. I had built an appetite for one thing; the Word of God. And, he was never too busy to sit and read, book after book, chapter after chapter, verse after verse to me for the entire month. Even when morphine and other heavy narcotics left me cloudy, I still managed to ask questions and find peace with God who was fighting even this battle for me.

Roger's devotion was new to me from a man; even from the best of them. I had learned to depend on him when my mom was in the hospital a year prior, but this was a whole other level, of stepping up. He handled everything I needed, which for me all revolves around my son. If Christian is well I am well. He made sure my son was taken care of and he managed to run his company from my bedside while asking questions, watching nurses, and meeting with my doctors, for the entire month. I never once felt alone. I *knew* that God was there, but to feel His presence in someone else whose there, in the natural, was yet another miracle for me.

We were both committed to celibacy till marriage so the stepping up for me, and the devotion he had to me, were mind blowing because it was purely about, me. He loved me, my smile, my laugh, my mind, my heart; me. I have been loved by men absent sex before, but never as intentional and committed to making me their wife, as Roger was. A man I was in a love relationship with always expected that sex was part of things. For that matter so did I. Sadly, in that month in the hospital, as my knowledge of the Word grew, I grew to realize how many men I had given myself, my love, my help, my time, and my resources to without even a fraction of this type of devotion and commitment. I thought of the years I had thought I was in control of my body, and my heart. I had just played the game Satan wanted, thinking I was winning, while not recognizing the game had played me and stolen years of my life from me. I, like all women, deserve partnership. Its what we are made for.

Even after being saved, it took me years of dating in the wrong way to surrender and commit to doing it God's way. It took me years to actually accept that sex before marriage is wrong, and to see *why* it's wrong. I finally came to understand the many ways that God desires to protect us by telling us to save sex for the marriage bed. He is protecting our identity by trying to give us instruction about physical intimacy that we do well to heed. He has a myriad of reasons that we often cannot understand until we truly seek understanding, for why our purity brings an entirely different level of happiness and clarity to our lives. The multitude of issues we bring into a marriage because we've known other relationships, physically, is but the tip of the iceberg.

No young woman should feel surprised when a man treats her as the Daughter of a King that she really is. Sadly, she won't find a man young or old who will until she realizes that's just what she is; a daughter of The King. Surrender to this truth as fact, is the first step in allowing God to reveal His miraculous plans for restoration, and blessing, in your life. This was exactly what Teddy was trying to teach me at breakfast at The Peninsula years before, I realized. This is what he thought was so screwed up about my generation of women. He simply wanted to give me a gift, albeit an expensive one, to express his love and appreciation for me as a woman and a friend. I assumed sex was now part of the exchange for his tremendous kindness and affection. It saddened him deeply, I realize, because he wanted me to value myself enough to never assume that my being given an expensive gift could only be because he, or any man, wanted my body.

Rather, Teddy, as someone who loved me deeply, as did Howard, as did a handful of my other great guy friends, wanted me to assume that it was because I deserved it for the blessing of my friendship alone. I was enough and I was not just my body. I had been reduced so traumatically, at such an early age, to being just a body, that the scars of this had infected my entire life. As my mind was transformed daily, more and more, by Christ, I realized how much more valuable I was, not just to Him, but finally to myself.

The despair came in my present reality, however. I was here in a hospital, threatened with losing my life. I had the chance to finally do it right, with a man who was right, and now perhaps it was to late. Even surrendered to whatever His will was, I prayed deep in my soul, not to die, and to be able to walk this new life out living in these new revelations and possibly, one day, teach others about them through the many mistakes I had made. Honestly, I prayed to just be allowed to teach my son, and to make up for years of not being present in my mind fully for him; much less God.

I began to understand, through Roger, that partnership and marriage was truly from God, and possible only *with* God. The vows I was contemplating with him, before I became ill, were becoming clearer to me; what God has joined together let no man, not even me, put asunder. For better or worse. For richer for poorer.

In the two years of our friendship to the point I was in the hospital, life had already given us for better and worse; yet he loved me. Life had already given us for richer or for poorer; yet he still loved me. God, we both knew, definitely joined us together and even with the walls, the challenges, and the brokenness that still remained underneath my being saved, yet newly surrendered; he still loved me.

I knew we were to be married, but the depth of what that meant to God became clear to me for the first time ever. Yet as I lay in bed, unsure of whether I would, in fact, live or die, my revelations were stained by sadness, because what did clarity matter for, if not to live?

38

THE POWER OF PRAYER

LORD my God, I called to you for help, and you healed me.
Psalm 30:2 (NIV)

Christian came to my room one day on his way to a school dance. He wore an ill-fitting suit as most fifteen year olds do. He didn't really want to be in the room. He was staying with a friend while I was hospitalized because they lived down the street from the hospital and he was close enough to come see me after school. I could sense he was angry and confused and scared. I hurt so bad because I didn't know what to do so on that evening, completely desperate, I decided to ask him to pray for me. I was hopeful this would cause him to deal with whatever he was feeling with God.

Christian's prayer was the most incredible thing I've ever heard. He climbed in bed with me and prayed simply, "God please don't punish me and take my mom from me. Please heal her. Please." My heart dropped. I could barely hide my tears at the depth of my despair over him thinking he was, in any way being punished, by God.

We lay in silence for what seemed like forever. Then he prayed some more. Eventually, the peace of God flooded my room and permeated throughout every single pore of my being. I knew God would not do this to him. He would not allow this. I felt the presence of the Almighty and I knew without a doubt that I was healed.

I suddenly experienced a rush of calm that I had not felt in the last four months of knowing I was ill and trying desperately to get a doctor to find out what exactly I was ill with. As I held my baby, my son, whom God had given me in a prison cell in Italy, to save me repeatedly, I exhaled.

"Gods not going to take me from you honey. Your prayers are gonna be answered." He finally sat up and left to go with his friend, who was waiting in the car with his parents, to the school party.

"Roger, I'm healed." I said as he left the room. Roger looked at me and smiled. "No, you don't get it. His prayer. I am healed. I felt it. I have a peace that's crazy. I know what God just did."

Just then my mom entered the room and I told her what happened with Christian. She listened, as if she understood, but it was clear she was still riddled with worry and waiting for doctors reports and biopsies about my nearly two feet of intestines, and thirteen lymph nodes, that had been removed. We were scheduled to have a couple more days of waiting before we would know something. She was radiating anxiety from every pore.

The next day, not even twenty-four hours after Christian's prayer, my oncologist broke rank and came to share good news.

"I have amazing news from your reports." I sat up intently as best I could. Roger was all ears also.

"You had what's called carcinoid tumors. They're not carcinoma. Carcinoma is very aggressive. Carcinoid tumors are different."

"What do you mean?"

"I mean this is really great news. It's completely unexpected. It's the miracle in the world of cancerous tumors."

"OK." Roger and I exchanged looks. "Do I need chemo or radiation?" I asked, not really understanding anything except that what I knew the night before was true. I was in fact going to be OK.

"No, your tumors don't respond to chemo or radiation. They just need to be removed, which Dr. Essner did. Cynthia, it's sort of a miracle." He stated, convinced. "These tumors are only diagnosed five or six times a year here in America. And when they are, if they're removable, that's the treatment. You're going to be fine."

"I already know. Christian prayed for me and I've had the craziest peace ever since. I knew I was healed after he prayed."

The doctor looked at me curiously and then he smiled. I could see the happiness he felt that I was going to be OK, even amidst an inability to fully comprehend my faith in what occurred in the room when my son prayed for me the evening before. Christians prayer's were answered. God's assurance in my heart, that my baby boy would not lose his mom, was the second greatest gift I've ever been given. His birth was the first. The fact that I would be here with him to watch him grow and go to college, and pursue his dreams, and become a young man, and experience his first love, and his first heartbreak, are still the only blessings that truly matter to me that, God has been so gracious to allow. My Father's love has given me everything I've ever desired and it has all been found in my son. In the years to come, I would never lose sight of being grateful for the simplest things. Living each new day to see and hear from my son. I am often humbled at the gift God has given me to be his mother.

39

BROKENNESS

And He was handed the book of the prophet Isaiah. And when He had opened the book, He found the place where it was written:
The Spirit of the Lord is upon Me, Because He has anointed Me
To preach the gospel to the poor; He has sent Me to heal the brokenhearted, To proclaim liberty to the captives, And recovery of sight to the blind, To set at liberty those who are oppressed;
Luke 4:17-18 (NKJV)

Miracles of healing are something I have seen a number of times since my first experience with my own. In college at the University of Kansas, my son and his friends prayed for a deaf kid who got his hearing back in our living room after a Bible study one night. He had five surgeries with doctors from Yale to Harvard throughout his young life and nothing worked. Until that night, when God opened his ears. Three years later he's still sharing the gospel. Countless college kids, who came in and out of study, many of them student athletes and teammates of my son, all received healing from various injuries, on a regular basis.

But of all the healing I've seen nothing touches me in the way it does when I see an emotional healing, which in my opinion, can often be greater than the physical ones. The enormity of a child of God being healed of fear, or anxiety, or depression, or abandonment issues, is equally as powerful, and life transformative, as those healed from a physical impairment. Many times, even more powerful, because while the physical impacts the body and its ability to function at its highest, much can be said about the emotional wounds and scars that impact the mind's ability to function at its highest.

Brokenness, caused from traumatic events, usually stemming from childhood, can mentally debilitate an entire life. Worse, broken people break other people. So, the broken parts you carry threaten to damage not just you, but also everyone and everything around you, especially your kids, if you have them.

Sadly, this is often an area the church never fully comprehends the depth of. Yet, it's the reason why millions of Christians live lives feeling anything but peace that surpasses understanding, joy unspeakable, and abundance as promised by God.

Millions of people around the world spend money daily seeking help. They pay for therapists, psychologists, psychiatrists, gurus, psychics, healers, shamans, drugs, sex; you name it. They will give and pay anything for understanding, and freedom, from any emotional captivity they may know they're in. Most people don't understand *why* they're in emotional captivity, and if they do, they cannot understand why it won't go away.

Secular therapy can give you all the tools in the world, and psychotherapy can give you all the pills in the world, but there is only one power I have ever encountered that has completely set me free from the emotional captivity of my brokenness. I am not saying that some people don't need medication. I *am* saying that I have seen hundreds of people come off of medication, once Jesus permanently heals them.

As written about the coming Savior, He promised us in Isaiah 61, that He came to bind up the broken hearted and to set the captives free. Nobody else. Only Him. Only Jesus can bind up and put back together a broken heart setting you free from the emotional captivity of the pain experienced by it.

When the heart and mind are broken the damage is usually visible on the outside, even if misunderstood on the inside. Therefore, it is often made worse by the judgments, condemnations, and wounds inflicted by others, and by one's self. To go through life behaving in ways, and reacting to situations in ways, that you don't recognize as abnormal or extreme, creates a really lonely, isolated, fearful, and sad reality to live in. While ignorance can be bliss it really isn't in terms of brokenness.

Typically, as we get older and recognize our behaviors more, God seems to allow things to intensify over time so that our brokenness becomes less hidden, and more obvious, not just to us, but to most of those around us. Eventually, you are painfully aware that normal people might become angry for normal things, but you on the other hand, go from anger to rage in the time most others take to become simply annoyed or agitated. With enough situations, you begin to suspect that perhaps you overreact, but you can't control it when the emotion comes on.

People who've never been broken experience a normal range of emotional expression. However, you become aware that your insecurity, or neediness, or fear of rejection, or inability to sleep even, is fueled by something that doesn't seem quite within the normal range of controllable emotions. You become out of control when in an emotional part. When the part goes back into hiding you're fine. When it comes out, to drive the car of your life, you're racing down a speedway headed toward a brick wall once again.

When it becomes evident, to the one who lives with brokenness, that there is something extreme going on, he/she can often fully comprehend that his/her emotional brokenness is disabling them and destroying their life, in many, many, ways.

Some areas of brokenness are more obvious than others. For example, kids who've been sexually abused typically break during the event and can react in a number of ways. My husband counseled one man who was sexually abused as a little boy so he used to wear women's underwear to be near to something feminine. When his wife was around he was fine. But when he was alone and the memories would begin he would resort to the only way he knew how to cope with his fear and feelings of shame. Others can become sexually promiscuous, develop intimacy issues, or become confused and have same sex attractions; actually unable to be aroused by anyone except the sex of the person who abused them. I've seen some women withhold sex or deny their femininity completely by dressing down or becoming overweight. Some will literally stuff their feelings down with food. They'll hide behind weight so as not to draw male attention to themselves. Consequently, they'll often get inner healing and miraculously lose weight becoming healthy eaters for the first time in life. Some men will hate women. Some women will be so angry with men that they treat them with disdain or belittle them. They have a difficult time trusting a man or receiving love from a man, because of their underlying brokenness.

Imagine being in a relationship with people with these types of brokenness issues. The love they desire they will literally sabotage, time after time, because of their emotional brokenness. The cases go on and on. One young woman I knew took on the spirit of the boy that molested her as a little girl and from the day of her abuse her mom described her as *changing*. In fact, she began dressing like the boy who molested her. Eventually she expressed attraction to women and whenever she and I speak of her being with a guy she cries. She becomes the little five year old girl all over again. She is stuck in a broken emotion and in deep need of inner healing. God actually told me in prayer one day that she was abusing women each time she was with them because of the spirit of this guy that she took on.

One young woman that we counseled with was raped by a serial rapist in college. She came to us two years after the ordeal because she was experiencing fear and an inability to sleep. We, of course, thought it was some delayed reaction to the rape. However, knowing it's not us but God who speaks in inner healing sessions, we simply prayed and kept quiet, and let God speak to His daughter. We were amazed when the memory that came to her was of seeing her puppy dart into the street and nearly get hit by a car when she was a small girl. Her fear part had initially broken as a little girl for her puppy, not from her rape. This explained why she kept saying she didn't experience feelings of fear at all during the actual rape; even while handcuffed to a shower for hours on end. The part that was created to deal with fear had long been there and went to work protecting her from experiencing fear during the entire rape. When this part got healed, she stopped experiencing fear in general and started sleeping peacefully and unafraid through the night again.

Many cases are not about abuse and brokenness, of course. The situations where the initial trauma is far less, however, can be just as destructive and intrusive in a persons life. We have prayed with people whom God has revealed are riddled with *anxiety* because a parent left them in the car while they went inside the grocery store. This caused them an inability to sleep peacefully as an adult. Once healed, he reported sleeping a solid eight hours a night from that day forward.

Another person had brokenness around never hearing her dad say he loved her. In that prayer session she forgave her dad and got healed of feelings of low self worth because of it. Not even two hours later, her father called and said he really felt awful suddenly and that he just wanted her to know that he loved her. He even apologized for never telling her as a child. Now that's God! Sadly, you may wonder what to do about all these things. Even sadder, you likely comprehend even less than others do about how to heal your *own* emotional brokenness.

This is when we turn deeper into Isaiah 61. I call this truly good news for the oppressed and broken!

The Spirit of the Sovereign Lord is upon me, for the Lord has anointed me to bring good news to the poor. He has sent me to comfort the brokenhearted and to proclaim that captives will be released and prisoners will be freed.
Isaiah 61:1-3 (NLT)

The heart is the seat of the soul. It's the center of all emotions. The soul is your personality; it's the person God made you to be. When the heart is broken, wounded and hurt, it affects your personality. You just can't be the amazing and successful *you* God created you to be when you're heart is broken. This is all fairly simple to take in at this point.

When your heart is broken, by an event, you wall up emotions and set them aside, so as to cope with the day to day. Emotional brokenness leads to manifestations of behavior that are usually completely irrational and often ungodly. This can look like rebellion and sin to the world. So, you're judged and condemned and more pain and brokenness is heaped on top of you. Gotta love the church. The only place that shoots its own wounded.

But to God, who alone knows and judges the heart, this is why, many times, blessing and covering continue to come to people you might otherwise judge as sinful and rebellious. Only God is qualified to judge a persons heart because He is a good Father who understands the emotional wounds, injury, damage and pain that His children live with; usually unsuccessfully. Since, His mercies endure forever as does His love, I am so grateful He chose to cover me, bless me, sustain me, and provide for me, while I figured out that I needed inner healing. Being set free from the captivity of my broken emotional parts allowed me to return home to Him and to find my identity as determined by *Him*.

He never gave up. Yes, He saw the messes and mistakes and many times the rebellion that the world saw. But, He alone also saw the limitations, the wounds, the breaks, and the tears, inflicted upon His child that had caused her to behave way beneath her calling. As any good parent, He chose to guide patiently, lead mercifully, and punish gently. He never acted without love. He never spoke without love. And, He never stopped pursuing me without love. Love never fails. It never failed.

No matter what your life today looks like, His love never fails. He alone understands your brokenness like nobody else can, or possibly ever will. He desires to heal you from the emotional captivity your past holds you in and He is not limited by human constraints in doing so. His is a supernatural healing. He, the same Savior who died for your sins, personally promises it.

No matter how big, or how small, most people seem to have some kind of situation or event that has occurred in their life, usually in their childhood, that has caused brokenness. That brokenness creates the wounds that get fortified into strongholds in your life. A stronghold is a fortress where you can run to that, over time, becomes more and more unhealthy to retreat to. God wants us running to Him and retreating in Him alone. Yet, emotional brokenness always creates strongholds over time.

For though we walk in the flesh, we do not war according to the flesh, for the weapons of our warfare are not of the flesh, but divinely powerful for the destruction of fortresses (strongholds).
2 Corinthians 10:3-4 (NASB)

We are human, but we don't wage war as humans do. We use God's mighty weapons, not worldly weapons, to knock down the strongholds of human reasoning and to destroy false arguments.
2 Corinthians 10:3-4 (NLT)

Reading multiple translations of this powerful scripture is powerful. It teaches us that the weapons we fight with are not of this world. They are spiritual. They have divine power to destroy strongholds. We don't have to do it ourselves because we have spiritual weapons that will do it for us. But, you have to know what the weapons are and how to use them.

This is where inner healing falls short in the body of Christ. Most people, even leaders sadly, don't know the weapons of our warfare or how to use them to cast down strongholds. But, these strongholds that are created in our lives can run our lives completely, ineffectively, and destructively. They take us captive emotionally and drive every decision we make from a place of broken emotion. You have to go to battle spiritually to tear them down.

Inner healing teaches you about the battle process. You have to get healed to be able to fully return home to Him or to fully retreat in Him. You cannot allow your life to be driven by brokenness or you risk being driven into all the wrong decisions, places, and things. Those places and things take you away from God. At best you become the double-minded man the Bible refers to in James. At worst your entire identity can get derailed.

Such a person is double-minded and unstable in all they do.
James 1:8 (NIV)

The calling on your life can be thwarted or seriously delayed, and you will risk losing even your own children to the world, to Satan's schemes, and to the myriad of emotional abuse your brokenness will cause them. To walk in the fullness of your identity every stronghold that's been created in your life has to be destroyed. Inner healing is the process by which this was achieved in mine.

Think of a plate; a fine piece of china or a nice daily plate. It doesn't matter. Just imagine a plate. Now imagine after some runs through the dishwasher the plate gets some nicks and breaks on the edges. Then your kids bang the plate and drop it carelessly, a couple times, and there are more chips and breaks.

Over time, the plate isn't exactly the beautiful thing it was made to be when it came out of the box and into the world; but the plate still functions. It's fine for a lot of daily uses, where not a lot of people will necessarily see it. You and your kids, and some of your guests, can still use the plate and put food on it. However, it's broken and chipped and not as nice as it should be.

So, now what?

Well, with more time you begin to realize that sadly, the plate you once loved, just cannot be used for all its intended purposes. When special company is over you opt to use the new plate that isn't chipped and broken, because you know it will make a more powerful impact when it's set on the banquet table for all to see. It's more effective and appealing for the job it was created for. Eventually, even your family and friends, who may have really liked the chipped and broken plate, when you first bought it, begin to grab the new plate next to it. They naturally want to use a plate that's more appealing and has fewer broken edges, when they serve their food on it. Especially, when they grow tired of getting scratched, or cut, by the rough broken edges of your original plate. If possible, they opt for a plate that's not broken, that won't cut them, when they try and choose it. The unbroken plate is more attractive *and* functions better.

So it is with us as God's kids. We are like plates. The soul is our essence. It's our core. The plate, remember, represents your heart; which is the emotional and deepest feeling part of your soul.

Even with broken pieces, and chips, we can function fairly well, day to day. However, those broken and chipped pieces of your heart, which are sitting there inside the cabinet, have names. Names like, fear of rejection, sadness, depression, anger, anxiety, you name it. All of these make up the pieces of our heart that are broken off the larger plate of our lives.

Because of the scenario I described above, friendships are ruined, marriages are destroyed, jobs are lost, children are damaged, homes are torn down, and lives are lived in complete despair.

Everyone wants to be the beautiful plate that functions in the role it was designed to function in. Everyone wants to be the plate that is desired by everyone else. Everyone wants to be the plate chosen to be set on the table for special occasions. Everyone wants to be new and unbroken. Everyone. I know I did.

When my husband, Roger, gave me this cursory explanation of what brokenness is many years ago, before we were married, I knew one thing and one thing for sure; I was broken. He knew, as did I, that I could not be married successfully without going through inner healing. Much of how I reacted to things with him, as a partner, was driven by brokenness. That brokenness had set up many different and varied strongholds in my life. I retreated into these fortresses to protect myself time after time through the years. But now, even when engaged in anything with Roger that made me uncomfortable, feel unsafe, or experience anger and the need to protect myself, my fortresses were actively employed by the enemy against me, and against anything and anyone who was good for me; which included Roger. I fought, I hid, I screamed, and I retreated into strongholds that were created by my emotional brokenness to protect me, but were eventually used by the enemy to destroy me.

My entire life; the low self esteem, the pain, the sexual promiscuity, the drugs and alcohol I casually toyed with to numb the pain those few months after River, the fear, the hopelessness, the anger, the inability to trust, and the ease in which I could shift out of one relationship into the next when the going got scary and tough, was all because of emotional brokenness. Everything I had lived through was, in fact, driven by the domino effect of the abuse I experienced as a child.

That brokenness was all rooted in events, and traumas, concerning not only my childhood sexual abuse, but also my parent's divorce, and my being raped as a teenager. Because of never fully understanding what to do with the brokenness that was underlying the behavior that I knew was not me, my life spun out of control, took me to Italy, drove me to fame and success, and eventually exhausted me to a place of total surrender. I came to the end of myself.

I remember looking at Roger one day, a few years past the day I surrendered fully, crying about my son's teenage angst, and my fears for him as an unsaved young man, in the New York to Hollywood community of uber privilege I had raised him in. I knew the reality was, that my brokenness had caused me to not raise my son in the way I knew I should have, and I was afraid I was going to lose him. After everything I had surrendered about my life to pursue a relationship with Christ that I was proud of, I was afraid I was to late to undo the damage done to my son by my life of privilege, excess, and red carpets. On top of my incredible fear for my son, I was moody and always felt unsettled inside, even though I had lived as a Christian for years by this point. I knew that I wasn't experiencing an honest freedom inside and this was causing me to struggle with my faith.

In retrospect, I had been saved in mountaintop spiritual experiences. Angels spoke to me, accompanied by dreams and visions. My escape home from prison in Italy culminated, fifteen years later, in a complete absolving of my case by Silvio Berluscone's administration. I had lived a life of red carpets and privilege and fun like the majority of the world will never experience. Yet, all I could do that day was look at my fiancé, knowing that I didn't understand a thing about how to be free from the emotional pains I still felt inside.

To make matters worse, we were engaged by this point and I didn't know *how* to be married, or even in a partnership, with someone. I finally sat down and tearfully admitted my absolute fear that I must have been to broken, to hurt, to scarred, and to unworthy of truly being blessed with inner freedom and with God's lasting love. I explained to Roger that deep inside I never felt completely free, completely happy, or completely fulfilled, with anyone or anything. All I experienced were moments and seasons of happiness, but never lasting joy.
"I'm a Christian. I go to church twice a week. I love people. I treat others well and I speak about my faith all the time. But I don't get it." I cried deeply as I spoke. "I've gone to therapy. I have the tools to recognize when my issues are kicking in but why do I never get deliverance from the issues themselves? Is all I get, tools to *cope*?"
Roger looked at me as if he truly understood the depth of my despair and the point of my questions.
"I mean I don't understand." I continued. "Why bother being a Christian? What's the point? I speak to others all the time about His peace, and His joy, and why we need Him, but I don't have any peace or deep inner joy myself. I still hurt, and worse, I now expect that even with everything in my life going well another shoe will drop and everything, including you, will go away." Roger tried to interrupt me as I sobbed hysterically, but he couldn't interject.
"Where is my peace that surpasses understanding, Roger? Where is the abundance I'm promised in the Bible? If God is God, and He is real,

then is this all His kids get? Secular tools, from secular therapists, to *cope* with? Emotions control my day. I wake up in a bad mood some days. I wake up sad and down some days. Some days I wake up agitated and annoyed and fearful. Christian and I fight like cats and dogs, all the time! I don't get it Roger. I must be broken beyond repair. Maybe, this *is* all I get. And if that's the case why am I hoping in God and a bunch of seemingly empty, or untrue, promises in the Bible?"

All I could do was cry. I was so desperate. I cried. And cried. And cried.

Roger held me, and consoled, me and explained what brokenness is, as I've explained to you. As he explained the intricacies of brokenness and the way we act out because of it, and the way even the enemy will use it against us to keep us from our destiny by constantly destroying relationships and opportunity, I was floored to hear him describing exactly what my life, up to that moment, had felt like. To be understood brought a flood of peace to my spirit. I began to listen intently and to calm down. This was it. He explained how inner healing works and how it heals the broken hearted, because Jesus shows up supernaturally and binds up our broken hearts. I was suddenly filled with hope. I knew that this was a blessing that was mine, on the heels of my surrender. If Jesus could heal me and set me free from the emotional captivity caused by my brokenness; I wanted it and I wanted it NOW.

To know there was someone who understood, someone who could heal it all, someone who could set me free, was the greatest good news I've ever heard. Jesus had saved me in a prison cell in Italy, fifteen years prior, but this next level of saving would be the one that took me fully into my destiny. The calling on my life could now be walked in. This inner healing was a part of Jesus' ministry that He never gave to anyone else. Only He could do it. Only He *can* do it. Only He *will* do it.

I sure didn't need encouragement or prodding to run to the man, Jim Hanley, who trained my husband in this amazing area of inner healing. Jim and Roger were used by Jesus, Himself, to guide me through the technical work that put me in position for Jesus to heal me of one broken part after the next. This inner healing work saved my life, and completely transformed it. And, as they promised, based on scriptural explanation, it changed my son. Supernaturally, as I was healed of specific broken mindsets, created by my childhood traumas, Christian was healed of the same ones, or ones that had formed because of it. Why *Christian* you may be thinking? Well, he's what drove me. The exploding, moody, depressed, confused, behavior that I saw coming from him was terrifying to me and I realized that my brokenness had actually, directly or indirectly, caused his. That's how it works with your kids.

Brokenness had formed in him because broken people break others as I've said before. But most importantly, because the sin I engaged in, because of my brokenness, had given rights to the enemy, and opened doorways if you will, for demonic activity to come against, not just me, but my child. That's what your sin does. When you have children you give Satan the keys to tamper with their lives. That's why you'll see generations of alcoholics, or pedophiles, or rape victims. Drug users often experience kids who use drugs or become sexually promiscuous. And sexual promiscuity can often lead to worse forms of promiscuity and sexual perversion in the children of parents who've opened these doors.

Now understanding *why* I needed to repent, and shut these doors forever, I plunged into my inner healing work like a student desperate to graduate in one semester. As I was healed, the work of the enemy and the rights of the enemy to mess with me, and with my son, were broken, one by one. As my broken heart was made whole, Christian began to supernaturally change right before my eyes. Behaviors stopped immediately as I learned to take spiritual authority over my son, my life, and my inheritance. As my mind was transformed, I began to understand God's mind and His heart. I began to see and think about things the way He sees and thinks about things. I began to realize that I had been brainwashed since birth by TV, magazines, music, and entertainment into some very incorrect ways of living, thinking, and viewing the world around me and inside of me. As my mind and heart aligned with God's mind and heart for me, my son did the same. Today, I have a really cool, handsome, tall, smart, athletic, and kind, twenty-five year old that walks in the total covering authority and power of Jesus Christ. Inner healing is powerful. It affects everything and everyone around you.

I have now seen many lives changed and transformed by the power of Jesus showing up in the room, in a prayer session, and doing what only He can do. Lives, homes, relationships, marriages, children, everything that concerns you, is affected by you being made whole. Everything that makes you able to walk in the fullness of your calling is affected when He shows up and binds up the broken pieces of your heart. His healing causes an immediate restoration of your heart, to what it was meant to be, prior to a trauma. In turn you are immediately set free from being controlled by your emotions anymore. This process may take one session for some people and multiple sessions over a few years for others. I had some very complicated abuse issues, and for some reason, they believe highly creative people tend to break more, so my inner healing took longer. I believe that people who are more broken become highly creative but that's another book. There were times when I knew Satan was waging an all out war to not let me be free from certain mindsets. But, if you're willing to do the work, He will never leave you nor forsake you. Every promise He makes in His word is yours. When you get tired and weary just PUSH! Pray. Until. Something. Happens. God is not a man that He would lie.

God is not human, that he should lie, not a human being, that he should change his mind. Does he speak and then not act? Does he promise and not fulfill?
Numbers 23:19 (NIV)

God wants us to be in control of our minds and emotions. He wants us to make rational, prayerful, Godly decisions with Him while employing His wisdom. He doesn't want emotional decision-making driving our lives. We are supposed to be the boss of our emotions. They are not the boss of us. Yet, the world preaches, teaches, and lives in a self-indulgent fantasy by conditioning us to follow our hearts. But how can we?

The human heart is the most deceitful of all things, and desperately wicked. Who really knows how bad it is?
Jeremiah 17:9 (NLT)

I never understood this scripture until I understood brokenness and inner healing work. I always followed my heart. I was taught to follow my heart. I believed in the romance of the heart, and following it seemed like such a noble and grandiose way to live. This is what the entire world thinks. For these reasons this scripture never made sense. But when you understand brokenness, and inner healing, you realize that there is so much about your heart that is broken and misunderstood by even yourself, that following it is *absurd*. I followed my heart into one relationship after the next with the wrong people. I made decisions driven by a heart that was broken and splintered and operating at the childish age it was when I was first sexually abused.

You may be experiencing, right now, even as you read this, that He is employing mercy and patience with you. There are things that have happened to you, and things that you've experienced that you carry with you, and you know that only He alone really knows. That's why only He is fit to judge your heart. That's why I'm here to tell you to follow Him. Not your heart.

When your heart is made whole you no longer have broken parts operating independent of the core of the plate. They no longer pop up irrationally to drive you into an emotion you don't want to be in. You are a whole, new plate; free of chips and broken pieces and able to be used for all the special occasions God created you to be used for. When you are healed of the broken pieces of your heart, and the emotions operating your life, everyone desires you. Everyone wants to be around you, because they no longer get cut or scratched by your broken edges. You are safe to be around. And, you are ready to shine on the banquet table of all your dreams and for all the purposes God has planned for your life. After the news of a Savior, who died to free us from sin, and cleanse us to stand before the throne of grace, this is truly the best news ever preached to the poor and broken in heart and spirit.

Can you afford to go through life without this type of healing?

I say no. No, because I tried it. Albeit unknowingly, we all try it. We all know stuff isn't right when it's not right. And, no matter how hard we try to numb the pain, erase our realities, avoid thinking, lose ourselves in success and achievement, or distract ourselves with people and things, it's impossible to escape the reality, even in moments, that your life is out of whack when it's out of whack!

Even while running from God most people know they aren't running toward a better substitute. You may think you are because your flesh feels good in a moment. But, eventually your flesh hurts and aches all over again. It's an unending cycle of up and down and high and low with brokenness. Getting the inner healing you need for your life enables you to no longer run, but to live, and receive.

That's why, for me, this is the greatest chapter in the book of my life thus far. Of all the lessons I have to share, and all the messages I have to preach, nothing matters more to me than for you to understand that if you're broken, Jesus Christ came to heal you. Right now. Today.

Your entire identity depends on it.

40

FORGIVENESS IS KEY

Jesus replied, "Now the time has come for the Son of Man to enter into his glory. I tell you the truth, unless a kernel of wheat is planted in the soil and dies, it remains alone. But its death will produce many new kernels—a plentiful harvest of new lives. Those who love their life in this world will lose it. Those who care nothing for their life in this world will keep it for eternity. Anyone who wants to serve me must follow me, because my servants must be where I am. And the Father will honor anyone who serves me.
"Now my soul is deeply troubled. Should I pray, 'Father, save me from this hour'? But this is the very reason I came!
John 12:21-27 (NLT)

In discussing forgiveness there is so much to say. We could go on and on about what it is and means and why it's so significant. To simplify it for you I will say little but hopefully much about what's important to truly understand in your heart. God is too Holy and righteous for us to stand before Him without dying. In fact He told Moses no man can look on me and live.

But, he said, you cannot see my face, for no one may see me and live
Exodus 33:20 (NIV)

Jesus Christ died for us so that our sins would be forgiven, and we would be considered righteous, and *able* to stand before God. Absent this free gift of love you cannot see the Father. In fact, many who haven't yet accepted Jesus, describe feeling cut off from being able to pray or feeling a wall between them and God. That wall always comes down in the moment they turn to Jesus. They describe a great breaking free in the spirit. There is that moment of acknowledging your need for Him and turning to Him. In that moment we simultaneously find Him waiting; having already turned to us.

This puts into context the major reason for Jesus. He came into the world to die for the *forgiveness* of our sins. His whole gig was based on forgiveness. Why? Because, we *all* need it and because none of us could go before God without the supernatural cleansing this single act provided.

How then can we hold anyone in un-forgiveness? We can't. To do so is to make a mockery of the entire example established in the very life our Savior.

Thou sayest that I am a king. To this end was I born, and for this cause came I into the world, that I should bear witness unto the truth
John 18:37 (KJV)

"For this cause came I into the world." What was that cause? Why did Jesus, the Lord God Omnipotent who sits at the right hand of the Father, creator of worlds without number, lawgiver and judge, condescend to come to earth to be born in a manger, live out most of His mortal existence in obscurity, walk the dusty roads of Judea proclaiming a message which was violently opposed by many, and finally, betrayed by one of His closest associates, die between two sinners on Golgotha hill? I wouldn't have. You wouldn't have. But He did.

It was love for all of God's children that led Jesus, unique in His sinless perfection, to offer Himself as ransom for the sins of others.

We. Have. To. Forgive.

I had to forgive my parents for their divorce. I had to forgive my relative for sexually abusing me. I had to forgive the guys who raped me. I had to forgive Miloj for lying to me, abusing me, and taking me to prison with him. I had to forgive. But why? They were wrong. They didn't *deserve* my forgiveness. They deserved *punishment*. Yes, this is true. They did.

But, when you ask why; the answer is simple. Because, I too needed forgiveness. I too acted out, and reacted, and lived in ways that were awful before God. I was too sinful to stand before Him feeling blameless, without the covering and cleansing blood of Jesus Christ, which washed me white as snow.

"Come now, let us settle the matter," says the LORD. "Though your sins are like scarlet, they shall be as white as snow; though they are red as crimson, they shall be like wool.
Isaiah 1:18 (NIV)

I too needed washing from everything done to me, by me, and through me, that didn't glorify my Father's beauty and my position as His daughter. I now walk in the reality that my sins have been removed so far from me that I go to God in prayer boldly requesting and asking for anything I know is within His will. I never put my Father in a box because He owns the entire world and everything in it.

As far as the east is from the west, so far has he removed our transgressions from us
Psalm 103:12 (NIV)

You're only half way convinced that you can forgive the awful person, or people, that have hurt you. That's likely because you may not understand what forgiveness is and what it isn't. I know I didn't. Until I did. For starters forgiveness is not a Disney movie. The bad guy rarely lives happily ever after with the victim. If my child was harmed by someone I would not send my second child to be watched by the same person, simply because I had forgiven them. Wisdom must be applied.

Let's take a deeper dive.

According to Wikipedia, Forgiveness is the intentional and voluntary process by which a victim undergoes a change in feelings and attitude regarding an offense, lets go of negative emotions such as vengefulness, with an increased ability to wish the offender well.

In my words, forgiveness is giving up your right to judge. It's letting go of a person, event, or occurrence, and giving that situation to God to judge and deal with.

Forgiveness is different from condoning, excusing, forgetting, pardoning, and reconciliation. In certain contexts, forgiveness is a legal term for absolving or giving up all claims on account of debt, loan, obligation, or other claims.

OK now look at about 5 categories of What forgiveness is NOT.

Forgiveness isn't

1. Condoning......failing to see the action as wrong and in need of forgiveness

2. Excusing.........not holding the offender as responsible for the action

3. Forgetting.......removing awareness of the offense from your consciousness

4. Pardoning.........granted by a representative of society such as a judge

5. Reconciliation.......restoration of a relationship

Forgiveness won't have you stick around for more abuse. And, It won't have you declare something isn't wrong when it is. Forgiveness doesn't dismiss liability; it dismisses judgment and refuses to hold on a moment longer to a situation or person that harmed you. Forgiveness un-chains you and sets you free from the person or event that is chained to you with un-forgiveness. Forgiveness releases a harm to God and trusts Him to correct all things, rebuke all things, punish all things, judge all things, and make all things right. As He sees fit.

You will need to forgive, and in turn you will need to acknowledge all that you've done wrong, in response to a person, event or situation. By virtue of being broken by someone or something you will have sinned in response; even the sin of anger. Let the Holy Spirit bring to mind everything you need forgiveness for in prayer.

Then, ask God to forgive you.

I was sinned against tremendously. But I sinned much in return. I was hurt and dropped and abused and betrayed. But, I hurt others and dropped others and abused others and betrayed others. Jesus put it perfectly,

"I tell you, her sins--and they are many--have been forgiven, so she has shown me much love. But a person who is forgiven little shows only little love."
Like 7:47 (NLT)

When you get real with yourself about how much you need to be forgiven, every single day, you will fall more in love with Jesus than you've ever been. Since He alone knows the heart I would rather He know I love Him than view me as perfect. He died for the fact that we are imperfect, and His death was more than enough.

41

YOUR VICTORY LAP IS WAITING

Now I want you to know, brothers and sisters, that what has happened to me has actually served to advance the gospel. As a result, it has become clear throughout the whole palace guard and to everyone else that I am in chains for Christ. And because of my chains, most of the brothers and sisters have become confident in the Lord and dare all the more to proclaim the gospel without fear.
Philippians 1:12-14 (NIV)

This scripture powerfully describes how I feel today! I never have a moment of wanting to do anything in my life over because I may not have the many tremendous things I now have; my faith, my son and my husband. I do wish I had figured things out sooner because the longer it takes to get living fully for Him the longer you waste your time walking outside the identity He created you to walk in.

But, He has truly worked all things together not just for my good but also for the good of others. What has happened to me, as Paul said in the scripture above, has helped advance the gospel of Jesus; not just in me but all around me. He has used my trials and challenges as an illustration of that which is common to man. And, He uses the lessons I've learned to teach others about recognizing their own brokenness and about overcoming a variety of abuses and abusive behavior. He does all this because I've been willing to live as a Daughter. I've been willing to receive my inheritances and walk in His promises. I've been willing to trust Him by allowing Him to shape and transform my mind, my heart, and my life. He is looking for your willingness.

Clearly, the willingness is the pre-requisite because it certainly wasn't me being perfect, or mature, or even on time, that has caused Him to use me. I was willing while imperfect. I was willing while spiritually immature. I was willing while delayed, and behind schedule, with lessons I should have learned the first two times I read the Bible and not the last four, perhaps. But He got me here. He walked me into my identity by constantly pursuing me with His love, and often with His Fatherly rebuke, because I remained willing to be His vessel. You must be willing.

I would never have thought, looking over my life thus far, that I would be running an international women's ministry that brings television programs about walking your life out with faith, to women around the world. I was willing. He gifted me uniquely with the skill set for what I do, and once submitted to Him, He was able to teach me why He gave me that skill set, and escort me into my purpose serving His kids around the world; especially His Daughters.

Today, walking fully in my identity as a Daughter of The King, I am living out my dreams. On the countless TV shows I hosted, I longed to impact women the way Joyce Meyer, Marilyn Hickey, Paula White, and TD Jakes were impacting me. For many years as a baby Christian I watched these heroes of mine and loved how God used them to help me grow. I found the way in which God used their gifts to be so worthy of respect, because they were providing living waters to people, and not just chit chat about nothing, as I felt I was a part of providing on secular network Television. In many ways you could say I had the world's apple, but I knew it was bitter. All the while, I was looking into the garden knowing that I would trade that bitter apple for any piece of the sweet fruit growing in Eden. Any Daughter would. Any Daughter will.

The program tag line for my Sessions TV programs today is that they are 'not just another talkshow... but a walkshow' teaching women everywhere how to walk out their lives with Jesus as their guide. What I hope to communicate from my heart through my tv ministry is that I simply do not believe you can strip the real *answer* away from women's questions anymore.

The self esteem we need today, the authenticity we need today, the love we need today, the partnership we need today, the answers we need today, are all found in our identity in Christ. We are daughters, and sons, of a King and He has a plan for our lives. Period. To try and give you solely my advice, my shared experiences, or my opinion, are to deny you the power of the real truth that will change and heal your life forever. The wisdom from which I speak is not my own. Read Proverbs, or any other book in the Bible, and sit before the throne of grace seeking wisdom, and you too will become a fountain of wise advice. However, in giving that advice, even on a secular talk show, you have to acknowledge Jesus because He's the greatest takeaway from any segment on any issue. He's true power to change and that's why women watch these shows in the first place. They want to change. They want a better life. Peoples hearts and lives are broken and many feel held bondage to the brokenness of their past. Only He came to bind up the broken-hearted and to set the captives free. The anointing to heal, transform, restore, and repair broken lives, homes, marriages, kids, and careers, flows through the knowledge and power of God and the power He provides through Jesus Christ.

In my humble assessment of true impact, the world doesn't really *need* another Dr. Phil, or Oprah, or Barbara Walters. It *needs* a supernatural encounter with a living God. I have an inherent capacity to speak about Jesus. I *need* to be bold and vocal about Him because He's been bold and vocal about me. My hearts desire is that all would enter the Kingdom of Heaven. I know this is impossible. But I desire it, and I believe my desire is within His will.

I pray as you come to the end of this book that you will be inspired to chase passionately after four things; a greater understanding of your salvation and being saved, a commitment to prayer as you recognize the spiritual warfare around you and take authority over the enemy's attacks against you and your loved ones, the insight right now into revelation from God about your brokenness and the ability to forgive and seek inner healing, and a promise to begin to walk in your identity as a Son or Daughter of The King today.

You are beautiful. You are handsome. You are smart. You are fearfully and wonderfully made. He has *plans* for your life! Understanding who you are, and whose you are, impacts those plans greatly. A whole world is waiting for YOU to be revealed as His Daughter (Son). But the fullness of what the world gets depends on the fullness in which you understand your identity and are able to walk in it. Don't let another day rob you of your joy, delay His plans, or thwart the impact on the world that you were called to make.

Does your identity today lie underneath brokenness, a lack of salvation, un-forgiveness, or your refusal to completely surrender?

If it does, break it off right now! Repeat after me. Yell out to God, "Father, forgive me of my sins. I need, want, and accept Jesus as my Savior."

Stamp your feet and tell the enemy "No more will you rule and run my life. In Jesus name."

Shout out your prayers of forgiveness. "God, I forgive and release all those who've hurt me and harmed me (run the list) in the past and all those who do so today. I no longer wish to carry them chained to my life. I release them to you to judge and deal with. In Jesus name."

Cry out to God and take authority over the enemy whose speaking against your life even now. "Father, heal the brokenness of my past, set me free from these emotions of sadness, depression, anger, doubt, fear, and every other negative voice the enemy of my life speaks into my mind now. In Jesus name."

Now dance, rejoice, and sing, as you pray. "Heavenly Father, thank you for a Savior who makes me righteous, heals me, and sets me free. Today I declare to partner with you fully in growing in my understanding of who YOU say that I am and not who the world says that I am. The world doesn't know the real me yet. But now it will. I am a child of The King. I am fearfully and wonderfully made. I am more than a conqueror. I am loved with an undying love. I am the first and NOT the last. All things are possible for me with you Father. I am yours. You love me. In Jesus name."

Start walking in your power DAUGHTER!

42

IDENTITY AFFIRMATIONS

Every day remind yourself of who you are and whose you are! These are just a few of the things that YOU are. *This* is your true identity. *Own* it and get to work!

Matt 5:13
I am the salt of the earth
Salt makes people thirsty and more flavorful. What are we salt for? To make people thirsty for Jesus. He's a stream of living waters.

Matthew 5:14
I am the light of the world
You're made to radiate the light of Christ.

Mark 16:17
I have received the power of the Holy Spirit to do great works.
YOU are powerful beyond measure because of the Holy Spirit living in you

John 10:14
I know God's voice
He wants to speak to you. You have the ability to hear Him and dialogue with Him. Hello!!!

John 13:34-35
I have love for others.
Yes you do! You love because He first loved you.

John 14:12
I shall do even greater works than Christ Jesus.

He walked on water. He healed the sick. He raised the dead. And, He lives in you!!!! The same power and authority are yours? Wait a minute! What can't you do again? Repeat that. Right.

John 15:15
I am Christ's friend
Wow, think about that for a minute. You are a servant, yet God who created everything calls you His friend.

John 15:16
I am chosen and appointed by Christ to bear fruit
You are like a fruit tree. If you abide in him you'll just naturally bear fruit in your life and in the lives of others. Watch yourself blossom.

John 1:12
I am a Child of God (part of his family) (see Romans 8:16 also)
We are now brothers and sisters in Christ. Your Kingdom family welcomes you.

John 6:47
I have everlasting life
We will live eternally. We may not fully understand how but trust God and this promise. I will see you in Heaven.

John 8:31-33
I am set free
That's it. Right now whatever is binding you up, hurting you, limiting you, or challenging you, Jesus wants to free you of it. Isaiah 61 says he came to set the captives free. YOU are FREE!

Romans 5:1
I have been justified (completely forgiven and made righteous)
There is nothing you've done that He cannot forgive. Now forgive yourself and move on with getting to know your Savior.

Romans 8:1

I am free forever from condemnation

Tell the negative, accusing, voices in your head to shut up! In Jesus name. That's the enemy speaking condemning lies to you. God never condemns us. Satan does. God forgives us and saves us. Amen.

Romans 8:17

I am a joint heir with Christ sharing his inheritance with Him

Do you have any idea about your many inheritances? Get in the Bible now and check them all out. Google inheritances of God scripturally and see. Your Father owns the earth. Is that sizable enough for you?

Romans 8:37

I am more than a conqueror

More. Than. A. Conqueror. Bring. It. On.

1 Corinthians 1:7

I do not lack any spiritual gift

Anything he or she can do YOU can do too. And in your own unique way!

1 Corinthians 2:16

I have been given the mind of Christ

I was created to think like God? Yep. Your mind is as big as the Creator's mind. If you stay deep in thoughts of Him, He will release His thoughts to you and through you. He will let you in on the secrets of the universe. Amazing!

1 Corinthians 3:16, 6:19

I am a temple (home) of God. His Spirit dwells in me.

Soooo, do you wanna mix drugs, fear, sex, and all kinds of junk that harms you and defiles you inside God's temple?! I don't think so!

1 Corinthians 6:19-20

I have been bought with a price. I am not my own. I belong to God.
Drop the mic. He paid with His life for you. He owns you. You belong to Him. It's like being owned by a perfect boss who gives you your freedom and then tells you He will do all the work He bought you to do in exchange. *Whaaaat?!*

2 Corinthians 2:14

I always triumph in Christ
Do you hear that? Always! Not just last time or maybe next time. Always. All the time YOU win! Can you hear the song now? *All I do is win, win, win, no matter what?!*

2 Corinthians 5:17

I am a new creation (new person)
Tell all your haters to stop focusing on your past. You've literally been born again. You're a new person. Stop dwelling on yesterday's failures and disappointments. Jesus now runs the show! It's a new day in your life.

2 Corinthians 5:20

I am an ambassador for Christ
That's right. Everywhere you go you are God's girl, or guy. Represent Him well. The world is watching.

2 Corinthians 5:21

I have been made righteous
Yes, YOU are righteous. But what about that stuff I did you're thinking? Jesus says, "I took it to the cross. What about it?" His righteousness is now attributed to you as your own.

Galatians 2:20

I have been crucified with Christ & it is no longer I who live, but Christ lives in me. (I am now living Christ's life.)

Yeah, life with God living inside you! Wild and wonderful. Can you sing 'anything you can do I can do better?!'

Ephesians 1:6
I am accepted in Christ
If you've ever felt rejected understand that God doesn't reject anyone. People do. Put cotton balls in your ears so you can't hear the haters and go to God and get loved. He's waiting.

Ephesians 1:13-14
I have been given the Holy Spirit as a pledge guaranteeing my inheritance to come
That's right God left a will with YOUR name on it! And guess what? Your Father is RICH!

Ephesians 1:3
I have been blessed with every spiritual blessing
If you haven't started claiming them you better get busy. We have tons of spiritual blessing promises.

Ephesians 1:4
I have been chosen before the foundation of the world to be Holy and without blame before Him
They can say what they want about you but you were chosen to be pure and perfect before Him.

Ephesians 1:5
I was predestined (determined by God) to be adopted as His son or daughter
So He chose you before you got here! You can run your whole life from Him but if He chose you why not just accept it?! He's God. He's gonna win. You don't stand a chance. Daddy's home and He's got plans for you!

Ephesians 1:7-8

I have been redeemed, forgiven, and am a recipient of His lavish grace
Hey do you know what GRACE is? It's unmerited, undeserved, favor.

Ephesians 2:10

I am God's workmanship, created in Christ Jesus to do His work that he planned beforehand that I should do.
So you were not born without purpose and without work to do daughter! Get it together. Time to get busy! As RuPaul says *'Work'*

Ephesians 2:18

I have direct access to God through the Holy Spirit
The Holy Spirit is your gift for accepting Jesus as your Savior. The Holy Spirit will lead you into all truth. Just listen. He's inside you speaking in soft whispers. He tells you what's right and what's wrong. He's the one who convicts you of sin. Yeah, you guessed it, He's the buzz killer. But hey He looooves you and is giving you direct access to God so God can speak through Him into your spirit and be a parent. Parents always know when their kids are in trouble. He's just doing His job kids.

Ephesians 2:19

I am a fellow citizen with the rest of God's people in His family
That's right you have a powerful crew. And, we need YOU.

Ephesians 2:20

I am built on the foundations of the apostles and Prophets, with Christ Jesus himself as the chief Cornerstone
Dang. That's what I call a family tree!

Ephesians 2:5

I have been made alive together with Christ
Well, who can kill you or hurt you for real?!

Ephesians 2:6

I have been raised up and seated with Christ in heaven
Right now you're seated in heaven because you've been spiritually born and your spirit goes up to heaven before God along with your prayers.

Ephesians 3:12

I may approach God with boldness, freedom, and confidence
I don't know about you, but I'm going see my Dad about everything, anytime, all the time. He always comes through!

Ephesians 4:24

I am righteous and holy
Your sin may have made you feel unrighteous, unholy, and unworthy, but the day you accepted Jesus is the day you took on his righteousness. His blood washes you clean.

Ephesians 5:1

I am his faithful follower
Let. Him. Lead. You can't go wrong!

Ephesians 6:10

I am strong in the Lord
Even if you feel weak, you can climb inside Him and He is always strong.

Philippians 1:6

I am being changed into His image
Yep, you are. I see you and you're looking better every day.

Philippians 4:13

I can do all things through Jesus Christ
Wait. Whoa. Hold up. That's right. YOU can do *all* things through Jesus Christ. Because He lives in you there is nothing you cannot do.

So tell the haters to get outta your way so you don't run them over while you're doing what they say cannot be done. Go!

Philippians 4:19
I have all my needs met by God according to his glorious riches in Christ Jesus
Whatever you need take it to Him and just wait. He is coming.

Colossians 1:13
I have been delivered from the domain of darkness (Satan's Rule) and have been transferred to the kingdom of Christ
You no longer dwell in a dark place. You live in a land of light and power. Enjoy!

Colossians 1:14
I have been redeemed and forgiven of all my sins (the debt against me has been canceled) (see Col. 13 – 14)
ALL your sins. Nothing was too bad or ugly. He forgave you and forgives you. Send that guilt straight to hell!

Colossians 1:27
Christ himself is in me
Yeah you get it. The devil just got evicted. The house belongs to The King.

Colossians 2:7
I have been firmly rooted in Christ and I am now being built up in Him
You're getting better every day!

Colossians 2:10
I have been made complete in Christ
You don't need the world's validation. You don't need a like on your Instagram page, or a thumbs up on your Facebook page. You are sufficiently complete within Him.

Colossians 2:12-13
I have been buried, raised, and made alive with Christ
The old you is dead. The new you lives. The life in you is no longer your own but Jesus Christ's.'

Colossians 2:6
I walk in Christ Jesus
He orders your footsteps so keep putting one foot in front of the other. He will get you where you need to go!

Colossians 3:12
I am chosen of God, holy, and dearly loved
Repeat after me! "So, yeah, what was that you *said* about me? You don't want to work with me? You don't *like* me? You don't choose me for your team? Ha! Do you know who I am?!"

1 Thessalonians 1:4
I am chosen and dearly loved by God
Did you not hear me last time?! Keep it up and my dad is gonna get your dad and kick his butt!

1 Thessalonians 5:5
I am a son (daughter) of light and not of darkness
You don't do dark things. That's not you anymore. You live in the light. Get back over here kid!

2 Timothy 1:7
I have been given a spirit of power, love, and self discipline (self control)
You are not fearful, or inadequate. You are not hateful. You are not out of control and undisciplined for the job.

Hebrews 4:16

I have a right to come boldly before the throne of God (Throne of grace) to find mercy and grace in times of need

Feeling some kind of way? Take it to your Father's house. He knows you fell short. He's got you anyway.

1 Peter 2:11

I am an alien and stranger to this world in which I temporarily live

Ever feel like you just don't belong? Like the U2 song you still haven't found what you're looking for! Well, this is why. You're not from this ridiculous planet where right is wrong and wrong is right. Your soul resides in Heaven and lives in a state of perfection. You are just a sojourner here. Enjoy it, hate it, remain indifferent to it because one day you will return home and then you'll feel completely comfortable.

1 Peter 2:24

I am healed by the wounds of Jesus

Tell that illness to go! He's got scars with your name on them.

1 Peter 5:8

I am an enemy of the devil

Well, you better be! Because the devil wants to take you out. You are his chief target. So he needs to be enemy number one.

1 John 4:17

I am in the world as He is in Heaven

Meaning YOU can do everything he does in Heaven down here on earth. OK, now that's cool.

1 John 4:4

I have spiritual authority

He gave you authority in his name over Satan and every bad thing Satan does. Your authority sounds like this...IN JESUS NAME. With that name every knee will bow and every tongue profess that Jesus Christ is Lord. You've been deputized as sheriff of this earth in Jesus name.

Revelation 21:7
I am victorious
That means you will have victory. Watch.

Deuteronomy 28:1-14
I am blessed
You sure are. Wake up daily and count your blessings and your entire day will change. You will shift into power and out of weakness and lack. Promise.

Deuteronomy 28:2
I am filled with blessings
Everywhere you go you have blessings for yourself and others.

Psalm 17:8
I am the apple of my Father's eye
That's right Daughter. You are a Queen! Son, you are a King. He dotes on you. You are a delight to your Heavenly Father.

Jeremiah 31:3
I am loved with an everlasting love
You are loved with a love that will never fail, abandon you, or harm you. From now, until you die, and then beyond.   YOU ARE LOVED BY GOD!

Now Drop The Mic!!!!!! Peace. Out. Homies.

Hold on! One more thing! This is my favorite childhood prayer. I try
and live by this one. Just saying it opens me up to His presence.

Lord, make me an instrument of Your peace.
Where there is hatred, let me sow love;
where there is injury, pardon;
where there is doubt, faith;
where there is despair, hope;
where there is darkness, light;
where there is sadness, joy.

O, Divine Master, grant that I may not so much seek
to be consoled as to console;
to be understood as to understand;
to be loved as to love;
For it is in giving that we receive;

it is in pardoning that we are pardoned;
it is in dying that we are born again to eternal life.